Globalization and the
Theory of Input Trade

The Ohlin Lectures

1. Jagdish Bhagwati, *Protectionism* (1988)

2. Richard N. Cooper, *Economic Stabilization and Debt in Developing Countries* (1992)

3. Assar Lindbeck, *Unemployment and Macroeconomics* (1993)

4. Anne O. Krueger, *Political Economy of Policy Reform in Developing Countries* (1993)

5. Ronald Findlay, *Factor Proportions, Trade, and Growth* (1995)

6. Paul Krugman, *Development, Geography, and Economic Theory* (1995)

7. Deepak Lal, *Unintended Consequences: The Impact of Factor Endowments, Culture, and Politics on Long-Run Economic Performance* (1998)

8. Ronald W. Jones, *Globalization and the Theory of Input Trade* (2000)

Globalization and the Theory of Input Trade

Ronald W. Jones

The MIT Press
Cambridge, Massachusetts
London, England

This book was set in Palatino by Wellington Graphics, Westwood, Massachusetts.

Printed and bound in the United States of America.

Library of Congress Cataloging-in-Publication Data

Jones, Ronald Winthrop, 1931–
    Globalization and the theory of input trade / Ronald W. Jones.
        p. cm. — (Ohlin lectures ; 8)
    Includes bibliographical references and index.
    ISBN 0-262-10086-X (alk. paper)
    1. International trade.   2. Globalization.   3. Input-output   analysis.
    4. Factor proportions.   5. Heckscher-Ohlin principle.   I. Title.   II. Series

    HF1379 .J664 2000
    382—dc21

                                                                00-032425

for Kit

Contents

Preface

It gives me great pleasure to thank Mats Lundahl and members of the Stockholm School of Economics for inviting me to present the Ohlin Memorial Lectures in Stockholm in the autumn of 1997. This is an annual event, in honor of Bertil Ohlin who, following in the footsteps of Eli Heckscher, helped lay the foundations of what became known as the modern theory of international trade. This invitation provided me an opportunity to pull together various strands of my past research efforts on a topic of central concern to Ohlin, namely, the manner in which the traditional corpus of international trade theory can be extended to encompass not only the intercountry exchange of final commodities, but also the international exchange of inputs into the production process. My own purpose in this short monograph is to set out in simple theoretical terms new sets of questions that arise as well as some tentative answers.

I owe much to my coauthors of previously published articles that dealt with aspects of the material covered here. Thus my thanks go to Isaias Coelho, Fumio Dei, Steve Easton, Ronald Findlay, Henryk Kierzkowski, Sugata Marjit, J. Peter Neary, Frances Ruane, Roy Ruffin, Kalyan Sanyal, and Barbara Spencer. I learned much from this collaboration, and I appreciate the comments on the present manuscript that I received. As well I wish to acknowledge the many useful remarks suggested by a phalanx of colleagues and students, including Rajat Acharyya, Sven Arndt, Richard Caves, Alan Deardorff, Xavier deVanssay, Pedro Guimaraes, Carsten Kowalczyk, Greg Leonard, Bernie Munk, Michihiro Ohyama, Marla Ripoll, Andrzej Skrzypacz, Irina Solyanik, Morihiro Yomogida, and several anonymous referees. And, for continuous help with computational matters, I wish to thank Michael Van Roo as well as Jenny Smith for her expertise and patience in creating all the diagrams.

I acknowledge that at the present time there is a deluge of material appearing under the heading of globalization. Much of this work describes the recent trend toward greater levels of international trade and either applauds, on the one hand, or condemns, on the other, the consequences for less developed countries, the environment, the distribution of income within and between countries, and overall levels of growth. My focus is more selective and theoretical, concentrating on simple scenarios in which globalization entails not only greater trade levels but world markets in which some factors and inputs into the production process can be exchanged.

1   Introduction

At the end of the twentieth century, the volume and nature of world trade is much different than it was at the half-century mark, although comparable in some ways to what it was at the beginning of the century. One hundred years ago, the world was witness to large international flows of capital and labor migration (O'Rourke and Williamson 1999). Today there is much talk of "globalization," although the supposed benefits of it are sometimes disguised by the seeming damage being done by international capital flows, especially of short-term financial capital, in the "Asian crisis" of the late 1990s.[1] Technology today is incomparable with that of a century, or even half a century, ago. The costs of transport have plummeted, while the difficulties of communication between locales half a world apart have practically vanished in a manner completely unforeseen some decades ago.

These advances potentially allow easy commerce among agents in any part of the world but have done relatively little to alter the institution of nation states. To be sure, the Austro-Hungarian Empire and the Soviet Union have disappeared as political entities, and many nations have emerged from colonial status. The map may have changed, but it is still described by a maze of political boundaries separating state from state. Thus for academic economists, the field of *international* economics remains a vital discipline.

Just as technology has changed the manner and extent of international transactions, so have new ideas altered and modified the core content of international trade theory. In recent times, there has been the development of "new trade theory," with its emphasis on the possibility of increasing returns, imperfect competition, and intra-industry trade. Much of this work is, in my opinion, quite compatible with the more classical and neoclassical foundations of trade theory as laid down by David Ricardo, Alfred Marshall, Eli Heckscher, and Bertil Ohlin. There is no doubt that countries differ in their relative endowments of productive inputs, and commodities require different arrays of these inputs in production. These differences still account for much of international commerce, even if elements of increasing returns and imperfect competition are present. In an earlier volume based on his Ohlin lectures, Ronald Findlay (1995) renegotiated the terrain of modern trade theory to account for the basic *endogeneity* of the factor endowment base of countries, capital (physical and human), labor, and land, through the process of growth, education, changes in technology, and foreign investment. This book serves as a complement to this earlier work.

The hallmark of the discipline of international economics is its concern with the coexistence of markets with different domains. That is, some commodity and factor markets are international in scope, whereas others are purely national (or even regional), and the focus of the field is on the nature of the interactions between these markets (Jones 1995). Much of trade theory has been characterized by what is called the "classical paradigm," whereby (most) commodities can be traded in world markets, but factors of production and most inputs into the production process cannot. As I discuss in chapter 2, this view of the nature of trade when technologies differ among countries provides the basis for the law of comparative advantage. Where the existing core of international trade theory has been relatively deficient is in not allowing sufficient scope for the ever-increasing fraction of world trade that violates the classical paradigm since it consists of *inputs* into production.[2] The purpose of this book is to develop relatively simple model settings in order to investigate what changes in both positive and normative international trade theory are required by admitting trade in inputs. Although the concepts of comparative advantage and the arguments about gains from trade both survive, new questions can be raised, and modifications of old answers are suggested.

The scenarios I describe focus only on a part of what is usually considered the globalization phenomenon. Thus this book is not concerned with *financial* mobility of capital nor with instances of large-scale international labor migration motivated by noneconomic causes such as threats of war or persecutions. Instead, it maintains the attention paid by standard trade theory to *real* inputs and outputs and the susceptibility of their assignments to changes in market prices. As well, it does not attempt to develop formal dynamic models of trade and growth. Although this leaves out much that is of interest, both theoretically and in terms of current policy issues, it is challenge enough to realign our thinking about trade issues using simple models if the forces of trade liberalization and the fragmentation of production processes promote a greater international exchange of inputs. With trade taking place in both outputs and inputs, one issue I deal with at the outset concerns the question of whether these items are substitutes or complements. I then turn to an explicit statement of the basic set of production structures to be used in many of the succeeding chapters.

1.1 Are Commodity Trade and Factor Movements Substitutes?

Heckscher-Ohlin theory focuses on the roles of relative factor endowments among countries and the relative intensity with which commodities use factors in production. The classical distinction introduced by Ricardo and maintained by most of his followers has factors of production or other inputs trapped within national boundaries. Final commodities, however, can be traded, and one of the principal conclusions of Heckscher-Ohlin theory is that international trade in commodities could alleviate, at least to some extent, the discrepancy between countries in relative factor endowments. This will take place *indirectly* when countries export those commodities that use intensively the factors found locally in relative abundance. Importing commodities that would require relatively heavy use of scarce factors if they were produced at home is a means of relieving the relative scarcity of these factors. One possible consequence of such a trading pattern is that free trade in commodities could serve completely to equalize factor prices between countries that share the same technological knowledge, despite the fact that the factors do not have an international market. This *factor-price equalization* result, formally published by Paul Samuelson (1948), was also stated by Heckscher (1919), albeit challenged by Ohlin in his dissertation (1924) and later in his larger treatise (1933).

For my purposes, a variant on this theme is important. Is trade in commodities a *substitute* for the international mobility of factors in the sense that the volume of such trade would be diminished if factors were indeed allowed to seek their highest return in global markets? Much of Ohlin's treatise is concerned with factor movements as well as commodity trade. Credit for explicitly showing how the substitute relationship works out in a Heckscher-Ohlin setting is due to Robert Mundell (1957). His setting is one in which two countries share identical technologies for producing the same two commodities, and the initial free trade pattern reflects an asymmetry in factor endowment proportions so that the relatively capital-abundant country exports its relatively capital-intensive commodity, and the return to capital is equalized between countries. Suppose the labor-abundant country levies a tariff on imports that reduces trade without eliminating it. This causes the relative price of the capital-intensive commodity to increase in the importing country and, with it, the rate of return to capital. Now let (real) capital become perfectly mobile between these two countries. With the direct route of factor movement open to it, capital moves from the capital-abundant country, where its return is relatively low, to the labor-abundant country. Such a factor movement alters production patterns in each country. However, as long as each country continues to produce both commodities and trade takes place, the factor-price discrepancy is not reduced by the capital flow since factor returns are tied down to prevailing commodity prices, differing between countries because of the tariff wedge. The capital movement makes the importing country less dependent upon imports and eventually will cause those imports to dry up completely. However, this is not the signal for capital to stop moving, since relative commodity prices are still different between countries. Instead, capital keeps flowing to the higher-return country until the price of the capital-intensive commodity is driven down precisely to the level it attained in the free-trade equilibrium. This price fall becomes possible because the commodity has now become nontraded (behind the tariff wall), and the inflow of capital is increasing its local supply and thus lowering price. At the end of the adjustment process, the movement of capital has completely substituted for the previous trade in commodities.

Subsequent research by Doug Purvis (1972) illustrated how trade in commodities and mobility of factors might be *complements* instead, in the sense that opening up factor mobility could cause the previous level of international trade in commodities to rise. Purvis suggested that the pattern of trade might reflect different technologies between countries that happen to be endowed with the same factor endowment proportions. Suppose the home country has an absolute technological advantage in producing the labor-intensive commodity. With free trade, this commodity will be exported, and the country's wage rate will be higher as a reflection of its superior technology in producing the labor-intensive commodity. If, now, labor should become internationally mobile, it will be attracted to the home country because of the higher wage. The consequence is that the volume of exports will expand. Trade in commodities and factor mobility are complements in this case.

Jim Markusen (1983) discussed the general issue and concluded that if trade is a reflection of endowment differences (à la Heckscher and Ohlin), commodities and factors are substitutes, while if trade is prompted by other differences (e.g., Ricardian technology) commodities and factors can be complements. Even in a Heckscher-Ohlin setting, such a conclusion needs to be modified. Consider once again the kind of example provided by Purvis. Assume as before that the home country possesses a *comparative* technological advantage in producing the labor-intensive good and therefore exports this commodity. However, let this now *not* reflect an *absolute* advantage. Instead, if the general level of technology is sufficiently low at home compared with the foreign country, the wage rate at home will be lower than abroad. If labor markets are now opened up between these two countries, labor will flow *out* of the home country, thus reducing the volume of its labor-intensive exports. Factor markets and commodity markets are substitutes once again. As I emphasize in chapter 2, once international mobility in an input is allowed, *absolute* advantage becomes a concept that takes its rightful place alongside *comparative* advantage in explaining the direction of international commerce.

As suggested in Jones and Neary (1984) and Neary (1995), the specific-factors model provides an example wherein endowment differences by themselves are consistent with goods trade and factor flows being either substitutes or complements. For example, suppose two countries share exactly the same technology, producing two commodities with labor mobile between sectors and each sector making use of a type of capital employed only there. Furthermore, suppose the home country has a relatively large labor force, a small amount of type-1 capital, and the same amount of type-2 capital as the other country. If trade is allowed only in goods, the home country will be a natural exporter of the second commodity, and the rate of return to both kinds of capital will be greater than abroad because home wages will be lower. Now suppose international mobility of one type of specific capital is allowed. This will lead to that type of capital moving to the home country since its return there is higher. Should this be type-1 capital, home production of the first commodity would expand and trade would indeed be reduced—factor mobility would be a substitute for commodity trade. However, should this be type-2 capital, home exports of the second commodity would expand and trade and factor mobility would exhibit complementarity.[3]

Whether or not commodity trade substitutes for input mobility, instances occur where opening up trade in inputs or mobility of factors actually alters the *composition* of trade. Some years ago in his disquisition on Ricardian models of trade, Lionel McKenzie (1954) queried whether nineteenth-century Lancashire would export textiles if it had to grow its own cotton. Closer to our own time is the case of Japan, heavily dependent on trade for energy sources to fuel its highly industrial economic base. And there are countless examples in which foreign investment has been a necessary prerequisite for a country exporting mineral products (see Schmitz and Helmberger 1970).

1.2   Four Simple Production Settings

In competitive models of international trade, no single assumed production setting dominates the others. Although pride of place is usually given to the 2×2 Heckscher-Ohlin model, much use can be made as well of the simple Ricardian structure, or indeed the so-called model of "commodity exchange." As well, the specific-factors version of the multifactor model, as used informally by Haberler (1936) and developed formally by Jones (1971) and Samuelson (1971), is often used to carry through the analysis of the effects of trade on outputs and the distribution of income. I shall be making use of these production settings in

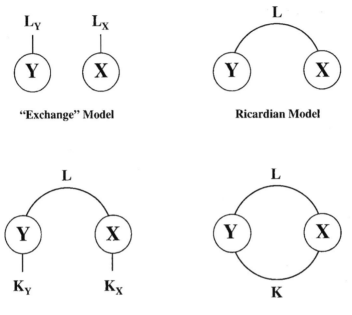

Figure 1.1
Four production structures in trade theory.

the succeeding chapters, and I illustrate in figure 1.1 a "bubble" diagram to display the difference in their assumptions.

Suppose in each case the economy produces two commodities, X and Y, in a setting of pure competition. The "exchange" model is often used to illustrate trade in situations in which commodities are not produced, they are just "there." But suppose they are produced, by two separate types of labor, L_X and L_Y, each fixed in amount and each specific to its own sector. This structure thus joins the Ricardian, Heckscher-Ohlin, and specific-factors production settings.

Figure 1.2 illustrates the production-possibilities curves for these four settings and shows two possibilities for the exchange model by the loci E and E'. As demonstrated in 1.1, the Ricardian model is one in which the specificity of labor to each sector has been removed. In figure 1.2, the transformation schedule is the standard linear form denoted by R. The two exchange-model-inscribed schedules represent the same total amount of labor, just differently allocated between sectors. In the specific-factors model one factor, say labor, retains its mobility as in the Ricardian model, but to produce each commodity a further input is required (denoted K_x and K_y), and this input is specific in its use as in the exchange model. Finally, in the 2×2 Heckscher-Ohlin model, the factor (capital, K, in this illustration) that is tied down by occupation in the specific-factors setting becomes freely mobile between sectors. As illustrated by Wolfgang Mayer (1974), the transformation schedule in the Heckscher-Ohlin setting is the envelope of various specific-factors schedules showing different allocations of a given total supply of capital (SF and SF'). Figure 1.2 is designed to highlight the analogy of exchange and Ricardian models, on the one hand, and specific-factors and Heckscher-Ohlin models, on the other. In succeeding chapters, I make use of bubble diagrams in relating connections between two countries, in which one or more inputs become internationally mobile.

1.3   Concluding Remarks

The rest of this book makes intensive use of these structures in discussions of competitive settings and is divided into two parts. Chapters 2–5 are primarily concerned with positive aspects of various scenarios in which input trade is cru-

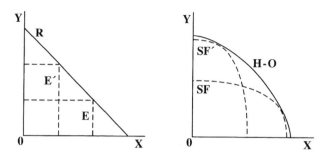

Figure 1.2
Production possibilities in the four structures.

cial, usually joining established trade in outputs. I have already alluded to the importance of absolute advantage once some inputs have international markets, and this is discussed more thoroughly in chapter 2. As well, the crucial role of a country's *hinterland* emerges in a standard Heckscher-Ohlin setting. Chapter 3 picks up the importance of this theme in the analysis of investment in foreign *enclaves*. A basic question can then be posed as follows: When international commodity markets are disturbed by changes in supplies or tastes, is there any presumption as to the subsequent relocation of internationally mobile capital? When world prices improve for a particular productive sector, does the degree of international industrial concentration rise or fall? How about the dependence of countries on international trade? Chapter 4 discusses the possibility that more than one input may be traded so that questions of choice arise. Chapter 5 puts center stage the production of inputs that enter international trade.

The remaining three chapters are mainly devoted to normative issues, leading up to concluding chapter 8's discussion of policy problems posed for national governments

when some of the inputs into production become internationally mobile. Chapter 6 presents a general framework en-
compassing both competitive and imperfectly competitive
market scenarios. Chapter 7 is both positive and normative
in content, concerned with the possibility that increased liberalization of trade and regulations, coupled with significant improvements in technology and reduction in the costs
of services, are allowing a fragmentation of production processes with a reallocation of the various segments among
countries previously unable to compete in producing the integrated commodity. The potential role for multinational
firms comes into its own in the fragmentation process, although arms-length use of markets may be relatively favored. Although competitive market structures are
maintained for most of part I, part II explores as well some
of the market settings and assumptions made in "new trade
theory," such as increasing returns, positive profits in equilibrium made possible by barriers to entry and the role of
services in trade and production.

My hope is that these analytical exercises in real theory
will provide for that branch of international economics what
past and ongoing work is doing for the financial and macroeconomic parts. The research that Mundell and others un-
dertook some decades ago has emphasized the importance
of financial capital mobility in altering the workings of open
economies and the policy options that nations have available. Here I undertake a study of the way in which real trade
theory needs to be modified once explicit attention is paid to
the fact that international trade and mobility is possible for
inputs and factors as well as for final commodities.

I

International Trade in
Inputs: Basic Theory

2　An Internationally Mobile Productive Input

The most simple way to begin the study of international trade theory when some input is internationally mobile is to analyze trade within the framework of an augmented Ricardian model. The "augmented" refers to the necessity of combining labor with some input available in world markets to produce one of two tradeable commodities. Although two inputs are required in the production process, the Ricardian assumption of rigid technology is maintained in the sense that all input coefficients are fixed. This analysis is followed by a more general treatment of the basic Heckscher-Ohlin setting in which two homogeneous factors are employed to produce a pair of commodities with flexible technologies allowing factor substitution, and one of these factors is mobile between countries.

What is the nature of the internationally mobile input? Several scenarios are possible. For example, the mobile input could be a type of labor that is specific in its industrial use. To push things back one stage, the internationally mobile factor might be a produced input, specific in its use and produced by a specific form of labor. To fix ideas, let me start by assuming that this mobile input is a form of nondepreciating physical *capital* whose ownership pattern is spread throughout the world. It can be reallocated in response to any change in its return from one country to another. Such capital earns a *rental*, and I shall often slip into different word usage and refer to this rental as a "rate of return." However, no attempt is made to link this with notions of time preference. Furthermore, I postpone until chapter 5 any consideration that current resources are being employed to change the world's supply of the mobile input. That is, the world's supply of the mobile input is taken as fixed.[1]

In the augmented Ricardian model in the following section, the scenario envisages two countries embedded in a large world economy, so that they are price takers both for the two commodities they produce as well as for the internationally mobile input. Following that discussion, I turn to a Heckscher-Ohlin framework but alter the scenario to consider a world made up of only two countries. Obviously all prices now become endogenous. However, since my focus is on the nature of the dependence of the return to the internationally mobile input on the relative commodity-price ratio, no attempt will be made explicitly to introduce demand considerations in order to solve for equilibrium price ratios. An alternative scenario can be envisaged, one that has more appeal if two countries in a many-country framework form a customs union or other regional arrangement, and as a consequence some input becomes mobile between these two countries but not with the rest of the world. If these countries were "small," they could then be price takers for commodities but not for the mobile input. Instead, I will stick to the setting in which there is literally a two-country world and investigate the dependence of the return to the input mobile between these countries on the commodity terms of trade.

2.1 An Augmented Ricardian Model

In the simple Ricardian model, a country producing two commodities—call them X and Y—would only use labor in production, and such labor could not leave the country in response to higher wage rates available in other parts of the world. Suppose, now, that to produce a unit of commodity Y requires not only a_{LY} units of labor, but also a_{KY} units of capital.[2] Both input coefficients are assumed to be fixed. Commodity X is produced only with labor, requiring a_{LX} units per unit output. Let w represent the country's wage rate, and r the rental on a unit of capital. In competitive markets the country's profit conditions, inequalities (2.1), state that in equilibrium no positive profit can be made producing either commodity. Unit costs could exceed price, but in that case no output would be produced:

$$a_{LX} w \geq p_x \qquad (2.1)$$

$$a_{LY} w + a_{KY} r \geq p_Y$$

Figure 2.1 plots the combinations of the relative price of commodities, p_Y/p_X, and the return to capital (deflated by the price of X), which would allow this country to produce both commodities in a competitive equilibrium. Clearly the higher the amount that must be paid for the use of footloose capital, the greater must be Y's relative price in order that this country can produce Y. Positive values for the use of physical capital raise Y's relative price; the slope of the cost line in figure 2.1 is a_{KY}. (Its inverse is the productivity of capital in Y production.) The basic Ricardian setting is one in which such capital is free so that the relative cost of producing Y is revealed by the ratio of labor input coefficients, a_{LY}/a_{LX}, shown by the vertical intercept of the relative cost line in figure 2.1. Thus both comparative costs for labor (the

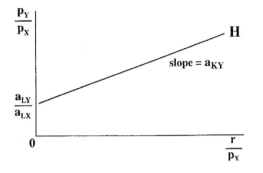

Figure 2.1
Internationally mobile capital.

factor trapped by national boundaries) and absolute costs of capital (the internationally mobile factor) determine the relative cost of producing the two commodities.

Refer to the country illustrated in figure 2.1 as the home country (H), and consider the cost situation in another country, the foreign country (whose input costs and wage rates are denoted by an "*"). It might be at a disadvantage as a Y producer compared with the home country in having greater comparative labor costs as well as less productive use of capital. In such a case, one would never observe simultaneous production of X at home and Y abroad. Figure 2.2 illustrates a different scenario, one in which a presumed foreign comparative disadvantage in relative labor costs in Y production can be offset, if the return to capital in world markets is sufficiently high, by a foreign absolute advantage in the productivity of capital.

The home and foreign country are assumed to be price takers in the world market, both for commodities and for the rental of internationally mobile capital. These two price ratios could be illustrated by any point in figure 2.2. If the

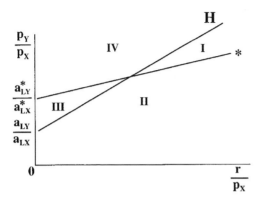

Figure 2.2
Comparative and absolute advantage.

price vector is located in regions II or IV, both countries would have the same trade pattern—producers and exporters of X in region II and of Y in region IV. In region I, the home country specializes in X and the foreign country makes use of internationally available capital in order to produce Y, paying its workers a wage higher than is consistent with the foreign country producing X as well.

The augmented Ricardian model usefully illustrates how the doctrine of comparative advantage, so dominant in trade models in which inputs are trapped behind national boundaries, must make room for the doctrine of absolute advantage for any input that enjoys an international market. A prominent feature of classical Ricardian thought is that low levels of labor productivity within a country do not preclude that country from sharing in mutually beneficial trade with countries whose labor is more skilled. Instead, low productivity is reflected in low wage rates. Alternatively, suppose that one country taxes earned factor incomes more heavily than does another, albeit uniformly over sectors. If no factor is internationally mobile, no alteration in trading patterns is required. However, such possible intercountry differences in taxation take on first-order importance in affecting patterns of production and trade if there exist any inputs that have a choice of country in which to locate. Chapter 8 explores in more detail how the international mobility of some productive inputs alters the options that governments can take in pursuing taxation and expenditure policies.

2.2   Heckscher-Ohlin in a Two-Country World

The augmented Ricardian model is, in a sense, a simplified version of a Heckscher-Ohlin 2×2 production structure. In this section, I consider the more common version of the Heckscher-Ohlin model in which two factors, labor and capital, combine in a flexible technology to produce each of the two commodities, X and Y. Home and foreign countries are once again assumed to possess different technologies.[3] This may be a matter of different blueprints, different climates (e.g., for agricultural products, or assembling aircraft bodies outdoors, etc.), or different skills of the national labor forces. Physical capital, again presumed to be mobile on the international scene, may differ in its productivity between countries, but if so this is attributable to the utilization of different capital-labor ratios or different available technologies since all capital is assumed to be homogeneous in quality. However, the mobility of such capital will bring about an equality in its (after-tax) rate of return wherever it is used. Finally, I now consider these two countries to be the only countries in the world. Between them, capital is perfectly mobile and the overall supply of capital to these two countries is fixed in amount. Although the equilibrium commodity terms of trade depend upon demand conditions, I take them here to be given parametrically so that questions can be asked and answered about (i) the endogenous location of capital between countries as the commodity terms of trade vary, and (ii) the link between the terms of trade and the return to internationally mobile capital.

The two extreme possibilities of very high and very low values for the relative price of Y are easy to handle. If Y's price is very low, neither country will devote resources to its production—each will be specialized to X. (Of course, taste patterns might require both commodities to be produced in equilibrium so that Y's price cannot be this low). In such a case, production for this two-country group assumes the extremely simple form of a specific-factors model in which each "sector" is a different country, producing the same commodity (X, at the same world price) as the other country, using "sector-specific" (i.e., national) labor and (internationally) mobile capital. The distribution of capital between countries (not its ownership, only its location) is determined so that rates of return are equalized. Such distribution remains unchanged until price changes allow one of the countries to start to produce Y. At the other extreme, if Y's price is sufficiently high that both countries devote resources exclusively to its production, there is again some allocation of the two-country world's supply of capital that will equalize its return.

Figure 2.3 illustrates the relationship between the commodity terms of trade and the return to capital in the home country if commodity Y is assumed to be produced by capital-intensive techniques. If the home country is incompletely specialized, the return to capital and the terms of trade are linked by section II (extended) of the three-part locus in figure 2.3. This locus displays the typical *magnification*

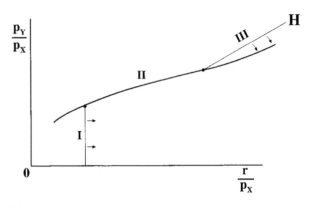

Figure 2.3
Heckscher-Ohlin setting.

effect (Jones 1965) whereby a rise in Y's relative price results in wider swings in factor prices and, in particular, on the rental on capital expressed in units of commodity X.[4] Thus if Y's relative price rises and both commodities are produced,

$$\hat{r} > \hat{p}_Y > \hat{p}_X > \hat{w}. \tag{2.2}$$

For any *given* allocation of capital to the home country, sections I and III suggest that for terms of trade that encourage complete specialization, the marginal physical product of capital is fixed in terms of the single commodity that is produced. Thus section I is vertical, and section III (which, if extended, would be a ray passing through the origin) shows how a fixed rental in terms of commodity Y becomes a proportionally increasing rental in X units as Y's relative price rises.

The foreign country is assumed to share with the home country that aspect of technology that makes commodity Y capital intensive, but to differ in the details that link relative costs of production to relative costs of hiring capital. Specifically, let me assume here that if both countries were to produce both commodities and if they faced the same rental on capital (in terms of X units), the relative cost of producing capital-intensive Y in the foreign country would always be lower than in the home country. To be sure, this does *not* imply that if capital were immobile between countries, the foreign country would in autarky be the low-cost producer of Y, since the foreign supply of capital could be quite scarce, leading to a high autarky rental rate. International mobility of capital rules out this potential source of difference in comparing cost structures in the two countries.

A possible explanation exists for the foreign country's comparative advantage in producing commodity Y, one that links its autarky relative capital endowment to technological superiority. Suppose that before capital is mobile the foreign country is capital abundant, and that some of this capital has been devoted to improving the technology. As a benchmark case, suppose the Hicksian degree of technological superiority, the improvement in productivity that would be observed at a given wage-rental ratio, is the same in both the X and Y industries abroad. Then with capital mobile, the foreign country must be able to produce commodity Y relatively cheaply compared with the home country (Jones 1970). The reason: Although the *relative* costs of producing the two goods would be the same between countries if they both faced the same factor-price ratio, the uniform technological superiority possessed by the foreign country ensures that if the two countries were to face the *same* rate of return to capital once it becomes internationally mobile, the foreign wage rate must be higher than that at home. As a consequence, the relative price of labor-intensive X must be higher abroad, or that of Y lower, once capital mobility is allowed.

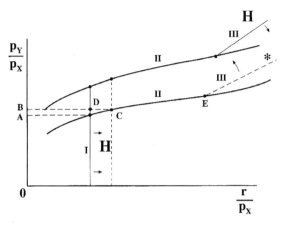

Figure 2.4
Capital flows from home.

Figure 2.4 brings the loci for the two countries together. In a world of capital mobility and free trade in commodities, an equilibrium position must reflect an intersection of these two loci. Given our assumption of a technological relative superiority in foreign production of Y at any common rental on capital, equilibrium must entail at least one country becoming completely specialized, and perhaps both so. The vertical section I segment for the home country illustrated in figure 2.4 is also shared by the foreign country for relative prices of Y lower than OA; the international mobility of capital ensures this lineup. Suppose the relative world price of Y rises to level OB. Before any reallocation of the world's capital supply, the home country would remain specialized in X at point D and the foreign country would start producing some commodity Y, with a higher rental on capital shown by point C. This comparison serves as an invitation for capital to relocate from the home to the foreign country. As capital leaves the home country, its section I segment shifts to the right because its rental on now scarcer capital at home is driven upward. The new equilibrium is at point C, where the new (dashed) section I home segment intersects the foreign section II segment for terms-of-trade level OB. Thus as Y's relative price initially rises on world markets, capital systematically flows from the home country to the foreign country, the country that possesses the technological advantage in Y's production.

All of this makes good sense as long as the foreign country remains incompletely specialized along its section II segment. But eventually the foreign country becomes completely specialized in producing Y. This occurs for two reasons: (i) For any allocation of the world's capital supply, the rise in Y's relative price encourages resources to leave the foreign X sector to be employed in the foreign Y industry. (ii) Additionally, the inflow of capital from the home country encourages more labor and capital to desert X production in favor of Y.[5] With reference to figure 2.4, the inflow of capital to the foreign country is associated with a counterclockwise rotation of its section III segment; at the point at which the foreign country becomes completely specialized in Y, the section III segment hits a point like C, moving northeastward along the foreign country's section II segment.

Figure 2.5 continues the story as Y's relative price rises. At terms of trade, OA, each country is specialized completely in a different commodity—the foreign country in Y and the home country still in X. A further rise in Y's relative price to OB would, before the subsequent reallocation of capital, once again raise capital's rental abroad to point C, a higher value than at home (shown by point D). The ensuing capital flow abroad shifts the home country's section I segment to the right and rotates the foreign country's section III segment counterclockwise so that the new full equilibrium (at

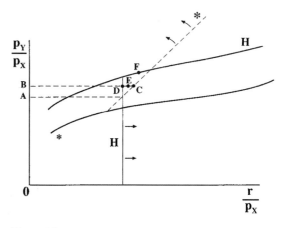

Figure 2.5
Both countries specialized.

terms of trade *OB*) is shown where these segments intersect (point *E*).

With further price rises for commodity *Y*, the home country will eventually become competitive in *Y* production, say at point *F* in figure 2.5. This is the point of maximum attraction of capital to the foreign country. Any further rise in the world relative price for *Y* makes the home country a recipient of capital previously located abroad! Again, consider the change in each country *before* capital gets reallocated. With the home country incipiently able to produce *Y* as well as *X*, and the foreign country devoting all its available resources to the production of *Y*, a further increase in *Y*'s relative price increases r/p_x by a *proportional* amount abroad, but by a *magnified* amount at home. (A ray from the origin, representing the foreign section III segment, must cut the home section II segment from below.) As a consequence, capital starts to return to the home country. This process continues until both countries are completely specialized in the production of commodity Y at a sufficiently high price.

Figure 2.6 summarizes the relationship between the terms of trade for commodities and the rate of return to internationally mobile capital in units of X. Clearly both countries would be specialized to the same commodity if its relative price is sufficiently high. In the intermediate range as Y's relative price rises from low levels, the foreign country becomes the sole producer of Y. Since it is incompletely specialized, the link between capital's return and the terms of trade is provided exclusively by foreign technology. There follows a range in which both countries are completely specialized, to different commodities. Now the *world* resembles, in its productive structure, the specific-factors model in which each country's labor force is the specific factor utilized in the production of the sole commodity produced (X at home and Y abroad), and capital is the mobile factor. It follows that in this range an increase in Y's relative price increases the return to capital, but not by as great a proportion. (And the wage rate abroad rises by a magnified amount, with the wage rate at home falling.) Once the home country starts to produce Y as well as X, home technology dictates that a rise in commodity Y's relative price drives up the return to the factor intensively used in Y production at home, capital, by a greater proportionate amount. Furthermore, as Y's relative price rises in this range, capital begins to flow back to the home country. This reversal of the capital flow is illustrated in figure 2.7.

The world transformation schedule for this case of internationally mobile capital is illustrated in figure 2.8. (I use the notation of putting tildes over variables to represent world values.) The changing specialization patterns depicted in figure 2.6 are shown along the world transformation

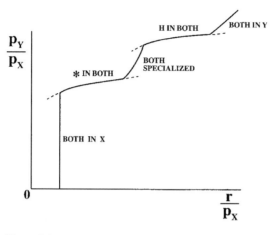

Figure 2.6
Price-return relationship.

schedule. Note the resemblance to such a schedule for a Ricardian labor-only case (not drawn). In the Ricardian model, world production possibilities are shown along a broken straight line. If the foreign country possesses a comparative labor-cost advantage in producing Y, it would be the world's first Y producer, and, symmetrically (for much higher prices for Y), the home country would be the first country to enter production of X—much as in figure 2.8. However, in the Ricardian case, relative costs remain constant as one country moves labor out of X into Y, whereas in the present case such resource reallocation drives up relative costs. In the Ricardian case, a range of prices at which each country is specialized to a different commodity and world outputs are fixed exists—those prices associated with the "kink" point along the broken line world production-possibilities schedule. Such specialization also takes place here, but in this range the location of capital can change so

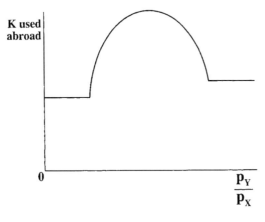

Figure 2.7
Reversal of capital flows.

that in the middle section of figure 2.8's schedule, world outputs of the two commodities change when capital moves from one country to the other.

2.3   The Chipman Flat

I have assumed, in drawing figures 2.4–2.8, that the technology of producing the two commodities differs between countries in a particular way—at any common return to capital, the foreign country possesses a relative superiority in Y production should they both be incompletely specialized. This need not be the case. Indeed, these technology relationships were drawn to cross in the augmented Ricardian model (figure 2.2); so also suppose they cross in this Heckscher-Ohlin model, as in figure 2.9. For ignoring this possibility in Jones (1967), I was (properly) admonished by Murray Kemp and Ken-Ichi Inada (1969) and by John Chipman (1971). In his exposition, Chipman reasoned that

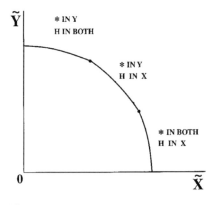

Figure 2.8
World transformation schedule.

even though there might be only a single commodity terms of trade that would allow both countries to be incompletely specialized in a world of mobile capital (as illustrated in figure 2.9), the world might, with finite probability, find itself with these as the equilibrium terms of trade.

Suppose, in figure 2.9, that both countries are incompletely specialized at point A. At those commodity prices, a movement of capital between countries moves each along its straight-line Rybczynski locus, albeit in opposite directions. Since the two countries have different technologies, world outputs change in a linear fashion. That is, in the case of incomplete specialization, the capital movement is consistent with the same terms of trade. In the world transformation schedule shown in figure 2.10, the linear stretch AB illustrates a finite set of world outputs at which the terms of trade shown by point A in figure 2.9 prevail. Thus there is a range of possible world demands that would elicit this given commodity-price ratio. In figure 2.10, the three-part segments shown on either side of the interior linear seg-

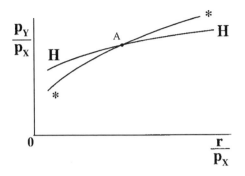

Figure 2.9
Intersecting schedules.

ment reproduce the kind of three-part segments of figure 2.8, with the roles of countries reversed on either side of the flat.

Figure 2.9 illustrates a case in which technologies differ but can nonetheless support an outcome in which both countries provide both goods and capital is mobile. Does the world supply of capital support such a possibility? As Yasuo Uekawa (1972) has stressed, such a result may be permitted by a comparison of technologies but not be observed in the world equilibrium, regardless of demand patterns. As I suggested in the preceding section, the given world supply of capital dictates a *range* of possible rates of return to internationally mobile capital, with such a range monotonically decreasing if the world supply of capital should be augmented. Thus the world might have too little or too much capital for a point like *A* in figure 2.9 to be included in the possible range of rental returns.

2.4 Concluding Remarks

The international mobility of an input into the production process (such as physical capital) alters some of the familiar

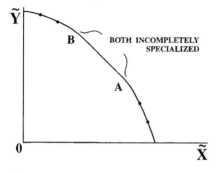

Figure 2.10
Transformation schedule with Chipman flat.

conclusions of standard trade theory. In the Ricardian model, augmented by the use of internationally mobile capital in one sector, the doctrine of *comparative* advantage in the use of each country's immobile factor (labor) no longer suffices to determine production patterns. As well, a comparison of the *absolute* productivities of mobile capital in the two countries is required, along with the return that each country would have to pay for the use of such capital. This implies that a world with some input mobility is a world in which trading patterns depend in part on country characteristics such as overall levels of taxation or regulation that may not be relevant (for production and trading patterns) in the classical Ricardian case.

The Heckscher-Ohlin model, as conventionally portrayed, makes a country's relative endowment of capital one of the crucial determinants of production and trade. International mobility of real capital ameliorates this difference between countries, although the assumed difference in their technologies and the fact that capital must be paid ensures that the model only goes partway toward resembling the

Ricardian labor-only case. Not surprisingly, the mobility of capital makes commodity specialization with trade, for at least one country, a more likely outcome. What may be more surprising, however, is the *nonmonotonic behavior of capital flows* as the world witnesses a steady rise in the relative price of the commodity in which the foreign country has a decided technological advantage. What I mean by the latter is that *if* both countries were to produce both commodities, the foreign country would always have a lower relative cost of producing this commodity once both countries have access to the world capital market on equal terms.

Under what circumstances would an increase in the relative world price of a commodity in which the foreign country has the kind of technological advantage described above lead to a flow of capital back to the home country (as shown in figure 2.7)? It is when the home country has a *hinterland* and the foreign country does not. A hinterland denotes a pool of resources or inputs used in *other* sectors of the economy. Consider the situation in which Y's relative price is sufficiently high so that the foreign country devotes all its labor force and whatever capital is located there to Y production, whereas the home country is still incompletely specialized to both. If the relative price of Y should rise from this position, it is an indication that the world wants more Y. To see what the direction of the capital flow should be to accommodate this demand for greater Y production, consider the following hypothetical question: What would be the response in Y output in each country should it receive another unit of capital. Abroad, the output of Y would expand by precisely r. At home, an extra unit of capital would also expand the *aggregate* value of produced income by r, since international capital mobility has driven the rental on capital to equality in the two countries. But this aggregate is made up of an expansion in the Y sector and a *contraction* in the X sector, which loses both labor and capital to the Y sector. The existence at home of a hinterland (i.e., the X sector, with its availability of resources that can be reallocated) more than offsets the technological superiority in Y production that would be possessed abroad if both were incompletely specialized.

A standard feature of Heckscher-Ohlin models is that factor productivities are completely unresponsive to changes in factor supplies at given commodity prices as long as the country produces as many commodities as it has factors. In the two-commodity exposition, this means that capital flows do not affect productivities until a country becomes completely specialized. Thus the potential role for a hinterland to affect the desired location of capital does not come into its own until one country is incompletely specialized and the other produces only a single commodity. The role for the hinterland effect becomes more widespread if the mobile factor is specific in its use and the number of factors exceeds the number of commodities so that factor flows have a direct effect on factor prices. The next chapter makes use of this alternative productive structure.

3 The Hinterland Effect and Foreign Enclaves

The idea that a region might have an advantage in attracting a footloose input into some productive activity if it has a relatively large sector producing other goods (i.e., a hinterland) surfaced in chapter 2's discussion of the Heckscher-Ohlin model with internationally mobile physical capital. The importance of this hinterland effect is more clearly revealed in a scenario that has capital being mobile between countries but nonetheless specific in its industrial use. Such a model setting, which displays more factors than commodities, allows factor flows between countries to affect input prices even if commodity prices are given.

I begin by discussing a simple model (see Jones and Dei 1983) in which a country is attracted by the possibility of establishing productive facilities in a foreign enclave, a region set aside by a foreign country for use of the home country's capital in an investment project, with labor supplied by the foreign country. Following this is a more general discussion (as in Jones 1989) in which two (or more) countries are analyzed, having in common production of a commodity that utilizes an internationally footloose factor (say physical capital) used in no other sector. If a commodity utilizing such capital experiences a significant price increase, is there any presumption as to how internationally mobile capital gets reallocated, or how countries compare in the responsiveness of labor flows to such a change in relative prices? Furthermore, what can be said about the volume of trade in this item as its price rises? As well, either exporting or importing countries may decide to tax trade. If so, how does the consequent realignment of the world's capital stock affect production and world prices? Normative issues concerning the desirability of a country interfering with input flows are postponed until chapter 6.

The chapter concludes with a brief discussion of a case that emphasizes possible balance in the two senses in which factors may be mobile—intersectorally and internationally. More specifically, in this case labor is capable of moving from sector to sector, but only within a country, while capital is sector specific but mobile between countries.

3.1 Investment in a Foreign Enclave

A simple setting in which to analyze the consequences of allowing the home country to invest in an enclave abroad is illustrated in figure 3.1. The home country is completely specialized in its production of commodity X. Its labor force is trapped at home, but its physical capital, although specifically used only to produce X, is capable of being relocated and sent to an enclave in the foreign country to produce X^E. Enclave production taps the foreign country for its labor force, while the bulk of foreign labor stays in the foreign country producing a different commodity, Y^*, with the benefit of sector-specific capital, K_Y^*. With X-type capital internationally mobile, its rental at home is equated to that in the enclave. I do not assume that foreign technology is equivalent to that at home or that the foreign labor force

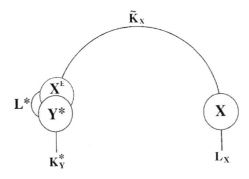

Figure 3.1
A foreign enclave.

necessarily has the skills possessed by home labor. In such a
case, the equality of rentals may well be brought about by
using more labor-intensive techniques in producing X^E in
the foreign enclave.

In order to investigate the sensitivity of foreign investment to changed world conditions, suppose that taste patterns change in world markets, resulting in an increase in
the price of commodity X (with unchanged prices for other
commodities). In the simple setting depicted in figure 3.1,
the hinterland effect guarantees that the home country
sends more of its capital to the enclave. To see this, suppose
first that no more capital is sent abroad. Then home wages
and the home rental on capital would both rise by the same
percentage amount as the price increase for the single commodity produced, X. Similar factor price changes initially
take place in the enclave before any further factor flows are
allowed. But this cannot reflect an equilibrium state of af-
fairs since the wage discrepancy between enclave and foreign country implies that more foreign labor will now be
attracted to the enclave, encouraging a rise in rental rates

there and a further inflow of sector-specific capital from the home country.

A surprising result may be in store for home labor: In the new equilibrium, workers at home *may* see their nominal (and real) wage rate fall even though the disturbance had been an improvement in the price of the only commodity produced at home. A less severe, but nonetheless surprising, possibility is that the nominal wage rate for home workers producing X (which has gone up in price) rises by less than the nominal wage rate for foreign workers producing Y^* (which has not gone up in price). This result follows if home production of X is capital intensive relative to production in the enclave, in the sense that capital's distributive share at home is larger. If markets are sufficiently competitive that the price rise in each producing region is shared only between capital and labor, any rise in the wage rate is limited by the importance of capital because the rate of return to capital goes up by more in percentage terms than the rise in X's commodity price. Hence, if capital's distributive share is larger at home, the wage increase in the enclave (smaller, relatively, than the price rise) must exceed that for home labor.[1]

The disturbance considered above was a worldwide increase in the price of X, leading to a consequent increase in investment in X production in the enclave. The latter result might alternatively be engineered by the foreign country levying a tariff on imports of X, assuming that enclave production falls short of foreign demand. That is, suppose investment abroad is aimed at providing X for the local market there instead of for exports. This clearly would serve to attract capital, and many instances have been recorded in which countries erect trade barriers in an attempt to induce capital from abroad to relocate within the country. Labor

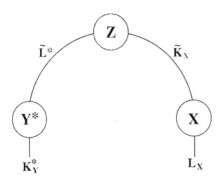

Figure 3.2
An alternative enclave scenario.

from the foreign country would also be attracted to the enclave. I focus now on the question concerning income distribution within the enclave in the new equilibrium. It proves convenient to visualize the scenario in terms of figure 3.2. The tariff levied on enclave production of X sets this market a bit apart from the world market for X. Therefore, I relabel commodity X^E as commodity Z and more symmetrically place the enclave as a region producing a commodity with capital from the home country (suited to Z production) and labor from the foreign country. A rise in the price of Z, engineered by the tariff, serves to attract both capital and labor to the enclave.

A bit of algebra is useful at this stage in order to ascertain the effect of the tariff-induced price rise on income distribution in the enclave. The way to proceed is initially to ask about the extent of the labor flow from the foreign country to the enclave as compared with the capital flow from the home country if the tariff (or increase in the price of Z) were to raise the wage rate and the return to capital in the enclave by the *same* relative amount, $\hat{p}_Z$. Consider the home country's demand for capital first. By definition, the elasticity of the marginal product curve for capital, γ_{KX}, compares the relative change in capital demanded at home ($\hat{K}_X$) to the relative change in the rental on capital, r (compared to the assumed fixed price of X). That is,

$$\hat{K}_X \equiv -\gamma_{KX}\hat{r}. \tag{3.1}$$

In similar fashion, the elasticity of demand for labor abroad, as of fixed supply of Y^*-specific capital, is by definition related to the relative change in the foreign wage rate (compared to the fixed price of Y^*):

$$\hat{L}_Y^* \equiv -\gamma_{LY}^*\hat{w}^* \tag{3.2}$$

These relationships reveal the relative changes in factors supplied by home and foreign country respectively. What is now needed is to relate these to relative changes in supplies available to the enclave. Thus:

$$K_X + K_E = K \tag{3.3}$$

$$L_Y^* + L_E^* = L^*.$$

This pair of full-employment conditions can be differentiated totally to reveal:

$$\lambda_{KX}\hat{K}_X + \lambda_{KE}\hat{K}_E = 0 \tag{3.4}$$

$$\lambda_{LY}^*\hat{L}_Y^* + \lambda_{LE}\hat{L}_E = 0.$$

λ refers to the fraction of each factor that is allocated to each industry.

To put these pieces together, ask about the conditions necessary to ensure that the wage-rental ratio in the enclave ultimately rises. This occurs if, in the above scenario, the capital-labor ratio in the enclave, K_E/L_E, should increase. Solve (3.4) for the relative changes in capital and labor supplied to the enclave, and substitute (3.1) and (3.2) (with $\hat{w}^*$ and $\hat{r}$ equal to the relative change in price, $\hat{p}_Z$, and the other prices, for home X and foreign Y^*, held constant) to obtain (3.5) as the condition required to ensure that the enclave tariff (or rise only in the price of the good produced in the enclave) induces factor flows that raise the wage-rental ratio in the enclave:

$$\frac{\lambda_{KX}}{\lambda_{KE}} \gamma_{KX} > \frac{\lambda_{LY}^*}{\lambda_{LE}} \gamma_{LY}^* \tag{3.5}$$

It should not be surprising to find that in this model with sector-specific capital the income distribution fallout of a change in commodity prices depends upon both factor intensities (as captured in the λ expressions) and substitution characteristics of the technology (represented by the factor demand elasticities, the γ expressions). Consider substitution terms first. Criterion (3.5) suggests that if the demand for capital at home is more elastic than is the demand for labor in the foreign country, an equivalent rise in home capital returns and foreign wage rates will free up relatively more capital from the home country than it will labor from the foreign country. The consequence would be a rise in the wage-rental ratio in the enclave. But this is not the end of the story. Suppose that substitution effects in technology are roughly equivalent in the two countries (i.e., the γ's roughly equal). Then the λ terms dictate the effect of factor flows on the wage-rental ratio in the enclave. Two interpretations of these λ terms are possible:

(i) *The wage-rental ratio rises if production in the enclave is labor intensive.* This interpretation accords with the traditional connections between factor-intensity rankings and the effect of price changes on factor returns. But to what is the labor-capital ratio in the enclave being compared? To *world* production possibilities. In the standard Heckscher-Ohlin 2×2 framework, a sector is labor intensive if the fraction of the country's labor force used there exceeds the fraction of the country's capital supply used there. Now substitute "world" for "country." If λ_{LE} exceeds λ_{KE}, the production of commodity X (or Z) in the enclave is labor intensive and a rise in its commodity price helps labor relative to capital.

(ii) *The wage-rental ratio rises if the country supplying labor to the enclave (the foreign country) contains a relatively small hinterland compared to the country supplying capital (the home country).* This comparison states that λ_{KX} exceeds λ_{LY}^* These two interpretations are equivalent, and their identity serves to link the concept of the hinterland to more traditional (but now reinterpreted) concepts of factor-intensity rankings.

3.2   International Mobility of Sector-Specific Capital

In the foregoing account of enclave activity, there was a basic asymmetry involved—the home country was the less desirable place to locate capital in the event that a price rise for X took place because the enclave had access to a fresh supply of labor, whereas by assumption the home country did not. In this section, I take a more balanced view. In principle, I could consider a trading scenario with any number of countries, each producing any number of commodities in a specific-factors setting: Each productive activity requires a kind of capital usable only in that activity, but with labor available to all, although trapped behind national borders. Suppose one such sector-specific capital is internationally mobile. Figure 3.3 illustrates the case for two countries and two commodities, a dimensional simplification that does little to distort the generality of subsequent findings.[2]

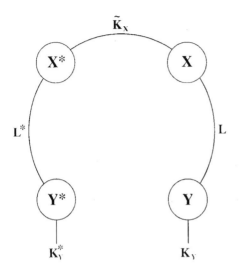

Figure 3.3
Sector-specific (X) capital mobile.

Imagine an initial equilibrium in which the return to X-type capital is equated at home and abroad. Technologies in the two countries are not assumed to be identical, nor are the sizes of the local labor forces or sector-specific Y capital. Suppose the world price of commodity X rises as a consequence of taste changes that shift demand from Y to X. In each country, a movement of labor toward the X sector occurs, and before any capital can be relocated, the real return to X-type capital would rise in each country. However, the extent of the rise need not be the same. If it is not, an equilibrating movement of X-type capital toward the country with the higher rate of return would be required. The question on which I now wish to focus concerns the presumption, if any, about the direction of the equilibrating capital flow. What is required is an explicit solution for the change expected in return to each country's X-type capital before the equilibrating movement takes place.

To probe this question further, I shall take an indirect approach by asking about the effect of the price rise on the wage rate in each country. If the wage rate should rise by a greater relative amount at home than abroad, a presumption exists that the return to X-type capital cannot rise by as much at home as in the foreign country, since both countries face the same price for traded commodity X. (Indeed, I am assuming that both commodities are traded.) The basic algebra revealing the effect of a price rise for X on the wage rate at home is standard, but repeated here. Equation (3.6) is the full-employment equation for labor at home, where input-output coefficients are represented by the a_{ij} coefficients:

$$a_{LX}X + a_{LY} = L. \tag{3.6}$$

For a fixed labor force, relative changes (once again a "^" over a variable indicates a relative change) in outputs and the intensity of labor usage are related by the following:

$$\lambda_{LX}(\hat{a}_{LX} + \hat{X}) + \lambda_{LY}(\hat{a}_{LY} + \hat{Y}) = 0. \tag{3.7}$$

λ_{Lj} again represents the fraction of the labor force allocated to each sector. Outputs are constrained by the availability of each type of sector-specific capital. Thus in the X sector,

$$a_{KX}X = K_X, \tag{3.8}$$

so that before any capital gets relocated,

$$\hat{X} = -\hat{a}_{KX} \tag{3.9}$$

Substituting this and a similar expression for the relative change in Y output yields

$$\lambda_{LX}(\hat{a}_{KX} - \hat{a}_{LX}) + \lambda_{LY}(\hat{a}_{KY} - \hat{a}_{LY}) = 0. \tag{3.10}$$

The elasticities of marginal product schedules have already been identified by the γ notation and can now be used to relate the relative changes in capital-labor ratios to changes in the wage rate deflated by the price of the produced commodity. For example, in the X sector,

$$\hat{a}_{KX} - \hat{a}_{LX} \equiv \gamma_{LX}(\hat{w} - \hat{p}_X). \tag{3.11}$$

Assuming the price of Y is unchanged, substitution into (3.10) yields as a solution for the relative change in the home wage rate:

$$\hat{w} = \frac{1}{\gamma} \lambda_{LX} \gamma_{LX} \hat{p}_X, \tag{3.12}$$

where the unsubscripted value of γ refers to the economy-wide elasticity of the demand for labor, a weighted average of the labor demand elasticity in each sector:

$$\gamma \equiv \lambda_{LX}\gamma_{LX} + \lambda_{LY}\gamma_{LY}. \tag{3.13}$$

That is, the term γ would answer the question: if the wage rate were to drop by 1 percent, by what percentage would the economy's demand for labor rise if capital is fixed in each sector (and commodity prices are unaltered)? A larger value for γ indicates that a country has a more flexible technology.

The solution for the wage change shown by (3.12) confirms that in the specific-factors setting a rise in any commodity price serves to increase the nominal wage rate, but by a dampened relative amount. It proves convenient to reconfigure the coefficient of the price change in (3.12) so that it equals the product of three terms—two of them referring to characteristics of the technology, and one of them to the relative importance of the sector's output in the national income. Thus, s_X can stand for the elasticity of the demand for labor in the X sector compared with the economy's overall elasticity of demand for labor:

$$s_X \equiv \gamma_{LX} / \gamma. \tag{3.14}$$

If technology in the X sector is more flexible than in the Y sector (or the rest of the economy), the value of s_X would exceed unity.

The extent of a sector's relative factor substitutability in the economy is one characteristic of technology. As all students of international trade theory are aware, another characteristic refers to the relative labor intensity in a sector. One way of capturing such intensity rankings is to compare the fraction of the labor force used in a sector, λ_{Lj}, with the percentage of the national product that is represented by the value of output in the jth sector, θ_j. If, for example, the X industry uses 20 percent of the nation's labor force but only represents 15 percent of the national product, X is labor intensive relative to the economy as a whole. Call this relative intensity term i_j. Thus,

$$i_X \equiv \lambda_{LX} / \theta_{X.} \tag{3.15}$$

Putting these terms in equation (3.12) yields as a final expression for the relative change in the wage rate:

$$\hat{w} = \{\theta_X i_X s_X\} \hat{p}_X. \tag{3.16}$$

That is, an increase in the price of a single commodity, X, affects the wage rate in a manner that depends upon the relative importance of commodity X in the national income as well as two aspects of technology. One aspect is the relative labor intensity in X production, and the other aspect reflects the relative ease of substituting labor for the other input used in producing X as compared with the comparable value in the other sector (or, more generally for an economy with many sectors, in the overall average for the economy).

Let me now assume that sector X is "typical," in the sense that both the degree of flexibility in the technology whereby X is produced and the intensity with which labor is utilized in the X sector are not much different from the national average. That is, assume that the product of the relative substitutability term and intensity term is close to unity, leaving equation (3.17) as the approximate solution for the change in the wage rate:

$$\hat{w} \approx \theta_X \hat{p}_X. \tag{3.17}$$

This leads to a commonsense result: If the worldwide price of X increases and two or more countries produce X and the quantity of sector-specific X-type capital available to each country is temporarily held constant, the wage rate in countries that are relatively heavy producers of X will tend to rise by more than in countries for which X does not represent such a large share of the national income.

The change in the wage rate in any country and the change in capital rentals are related to the price change for the commodity in question. For example, at home,

$$\theta_{LX}\hat{w} + \theta_{KX}\hat{r}_X = \hat{p}_X. \tag{3.18}$$

Distributive factor shares are indicated by the θ_{ij}s. Unless factor shares differ significantly between countries, the presumption about capital flows induced by changes in the price of X is that relatively heavy producers of X will lose some sector-specific capital to countries that devote a smaller fraction of their national income to X production.

The rise in the price of X "heats up" the local economy more (in the sense of driving up nominal wages) if it is a relatively large producer of X (as a share of national output).

This tendency of capital to flow away from economies that are heavily dependent on the output of X when its price rises results in a world X industry that becomes relatively *less concentrated*. Such a tendency is accentuated by comparing the labor flows in various economies. To pursue this matter, let capital supplies now be fixed as the world price of X rises. In each country, labor is pulled away from the Y sector (or rest of the economy). Suppose the home country is more heavily dependent on X production than is the foreign country (i.e., θ_x is relatively high at home). Then the *hinterland* from which labor is drawn is relatively smaller at home, and on that account a presumption exists that the home country's X sector attracts a smaller relative increase in labor from the hinterland than does the foreign X^* sector. Put a bit more formally, the response of the X sector in each country to a rise in the price of X depends on how much this price has risen *relative to the increase in the wage rate.* Since home wages are presumed to rise by more than in the foreign country, a presumption exists that internal labor reallocation raises home X output by relatively less than it does abroad. As a consequence, international capital flows *and* internal labor flows suggest that in "good times" the world's X industry becomes less concentrated than in "bad times" (i.e., when the price of X goes *down* relative to other commodity prices).

To the extent that such a presumption about the degree of concentration in the world X sector is valid, there is an important consequence for the extent of international trade that can be expected in times of both high relative prices for X and low prices. Assume that trade is more a reflection of disparities in production patterns than in tastes. Then in "good times" for X, the international flows of capital favor its increased location in countries that are relatively unimportant producers and that rely on imports. That is, the volume of international trade in a commodity whose price is rising might be expected to fall. In this sense, international trade is a "second best" method whereby a country obtains its supply of a commodity. In good times, it will tend to produce the commodity for itself, aided and abetted by international flows of mobile capital, whereas in bad times it will tend to rely more on imports from other countries that are relatively concentrated in producing the commodity.

The presumption argument utilized in the preceding account can also be harnessed to support a perhaps counterintuitive result in the event that international trade in X, the commodity in which sector-specific capital is internationally mobile, is taxed. The ensuing contraction in commodity trade in X could represent the consequence of a tariff levied by the importing country or of an export tax by the exporting country. What is the effect of either kind of restriction on the world output of X? The answer is that there is a presumption that world output of X will *increase* (Jones 1987).

The support for such a presumption rests upon an assumption that exporting countries devote relatively greater fractions of their national income to producing the export commodity than do the importing countries. If so, trade restriction, which induces mobile X capital to leave the exporting countries for the importing countries (where the rate of return on X-type capital goes up even more than the protected price of X), causes capital to move to regions that possess a greater *hinterland*. The result: Output in the importing countries rises by a greater amount than it is cut in the exporting regions.

The argument that trade restrictions induce capital movements that tend to increase the world output of the taxed commodity has interesting consequences for a standard issue in the theory of commercial policy. Ever since the writings of Abba Lerner (1936) and Lloyd Metzler (1949), trade theorists have been aware of the general equilibrium possibility (in models not considering trade in inputs) of tariffs or export taxes failing either to improve the terms of trade of the country imposing the tax or, alternatively, to protect the taxing country's import-competing sector. It seems legitimate to ask whether the presumed effect of capital flows in enlarging the world output of the taxed commodity tends to encourage either the Lerner paradox or the Metzler paradox. In part, this depends on demand conditions, since the capital flow can affect real incomes. I ignore this source of influence and concentrate instead on supply effects. The answer is that the paradox that becomes more likely depends upon which country levies the trade impediment. If the importing country taxes trade, the presumed greater output of the taxed commodity that is induced by capital flows would tend to soften world markets in this good and, as well, work against the trade tax protecting the domestic import-competing sector. That is, the Metzler possibility is heightened. On the other hand, if the exporting country levies an export tax on the commodity using internationally mobile capital, any induced increases in output in world markets tend to make more likely a deterioration in that country's terms of trade—the Lerner possibility.

3.3 Both Capitals Mobile

The schematic "bubble" diagram appropriate to the preceding discussion, figure 3.3, allowed for international mobility

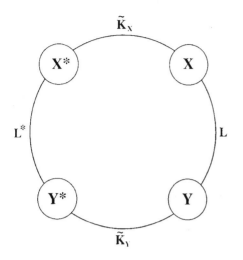

Figure 3.4
Neighborhood structure.

in only one of the two kinds of sector-specific capital. Figure 3.4 illustrates a more "balanced" case, one in which each factor of production has a kind of mobility: Capital is assumed to be mobile between countries, but specific in its possible employment to just one industry. By contrast, labor may move intersectorally, but is assumed to be employable only in its nation of residence. In such a case, what can be said about the effects of changes in commodity prices on the distribution of income worldwide?

The model illustrated in figure 3.4 is a special 4-good version of what is called the *neighborhood production structure* in Jones and Henryk Kierzkowski (1986). In that treatment, we first considered the case of a country producing many commodities, each of which uses only two factors of production. Furthermore, each productive factor has employment possibilities that are severely limited—to two industries. The

"neighborhood" label is suggested by the kind of bubble diagram shown for the case of four industries in figure 3.4;
each factor can find employment only in the sectors "neigh-
boring" where it "resides."

The structure of this model differs in a fundamental manner from that depicted in figure 3.3. The reason: Now the
number of productive inputs (4) matches that of traded
commodities. This implies that commodity prices uniquely
determine input prices; international capital flows do not
exert an independent influence on wages or rates of return.
To enrich the model, and to obviate the possibility that international competition would force some industries to shut
down, suppose that home and foreign industries in the
world X sector produce commodities that are not identical—they are differentiated types of that commodity that,
nonetheless, use a homogeneous type of capital good. (A
similar assumption is made for the world's Y industry.)

I do not wish here to go into the kinds of detail discussed
in the Jones and Kierzkowski article. Instead, let me focus
on one scenario: The world's taste patterns change in such a
fashion that the prices of X-type commodities rise by the
same percentage amount, while the prices of Y-type goods
remain constant. At first glance, it might seem plausible that
such a change in commodity prices would unambiguously
benefit X-type capital and harm Y-type capital, while the
wage rate in each country would rise in terms of Y-type
goods, but fall in terms of X goods. This is the kind of fallout
expected in specific-factors models, and such a result is possible in this case as well. Possible, but not necessary. To take
an extreme counterexample, it might be the case that in each
country the X industry is bilaterally capital intensive relative to the Y industry. Even so, it is possible that as X prices
rise the *real wage* in *both* countries unambiguously increases

and the return to X-type capital, which is used only in the world's fav- ored sector, does not. This possibility rests, in part, on the importance for the neighborhood structure of factor-intensity comparisons between outputs in the *same* world industry. Trade theorists dealing with the Heckscher-Ohlin 2×2 model are used to comparing intersectoral factor intensities between two industries that experience different price changes. Here it is the intrasectoral intensity comparison for the two countries producing in a common world industry and facing the *same* price changes that is important. These remarks are meant solely to whet the appetite, and they serve to confirm that analysis of trade in markets with factor mobility is made easier if the specific-factors structure, in which there are more factors than goods, is maintained. International mobility in a type of capital or other output, however, reduces the number of factors that have separate markets.

3.4 Concluding Remarks

In this chapter, I have stressed the importance of the hinterland effect. A price rise for a commodity produced in common by two or more countries that compete, as well, on the input side for a factor (such as capital) that is internationally mobile generally leads to a reallocation of that mobile factor between countries. The country with the relatively larger hinterland, the other region(s) in the country that employs nationally trapped factors also used in the sector favored by a price rise, will tend to have an advantage in attracting the footloose factor since the return to the nationally trapped factor (labor in our discussion) will not be bid up as much as in the other country. This led me to argue for a presumption that in times when the price of such a commodity is rising in world markets, the world industry tends to become less concentrated. This also had implications for the volume of trade. As the details of the argument revealed, much depends also on differences in the relative flexibility of the technology in producing the commodity in the two countries. The hypotheses about world concentration ratios and trade volumes when capital is internationally mobile are not truisms; they are capable of being tested empirically, but such work has yet to be done.

When less developed countries set aside enclaves in an effort to attract foreign capital, it is usually their cheap and available labor force that appeals to foreign producers, as well as relative freedom from local regulation. There is much about enclave activity that this chapter's discussion has neglected, such as the potential transfer of technology from advanced foreign production sites to the enclave or, what may be equally important, a transfer of knowledge about world markets, supply sources, and the nature of demand to potential local entrepreneurs. Additionally, local labor may possess skills appropriate to new technology, skills that need to be revealed by actual employment in the enclave. As discussed in Jones and Marjit (1995), the exposure to advanced techniques may help separate strands of the local labor force and help create greater wage disparities than would exist before enclave activity. In this sense, it may well be the case that increased international linkages bring about greater disparities in the distribution of income within countries.

This discussion has also ignored the possibility of increasing returns and agglomeration effects. As argued by Paul Krugman (1995), a pair of conditions is required to lead to external economies and agglomeration. The first is the existence of increasing returns in production. Although I have generally assumed constant returns in this chapter, I emphasize the importance of increasing returns in chapter 7. (However, there they encourage *outsourcing* or *fragmentation* of the production process, which tends to work counter to agglomeration.) The second condition is the ability to draw resources from other sectors. This ties in with the notion of a hinterland as developed here. One drawback of the simplifying assumption of only two factors used in production is that it obscures the important role in development and agglomeration of the existence of a wide variety of heterogeneous types of labor and capital. In the two-factor setting, an inflow of capital serves to drive down its rate of return. In a multifactor setting, an inflow of one kind of capital could well augment the returns to other types, physical or human. In their recent treatise, Masahisa Fujita, Paul Krugman, and Tony Venables (1999) stress the importance of the Dixit-Stiglitz (Dixit and Stiglitz 1977) model of monopolistic competition in which the appearance of a wider variety of inputs leads to increasing returns. Countries that have sizable industrial bases may have an advantage in attracting new capital, since the heterogeneity of the existing human and physical stock may provide precisely the kind of "hinterland" that this chapter has argued yields such an advantage.

As a final note, traditional trade theory has been frequently criticized for exploiting models with only two productive inputs—say, labor and capital—or labor and land. In our setting in which some input(s) is footloose on world markets, the small number "two" has a natural role in describing the input setting. Commodities are produced with two (sets of) inputs—nationally trapped factors (such as labor) and internationally mobile factors (such as sector-specific capital). This focus will be emphasized in chapter 5's discussion of trade in "middle products."

4   Choice in Trade and Input Mobility

The preceding chapters have discussed input mobility when only one input or factor was involved. I turn now to two instances in which *choice* becomes an issue for a country's policymakers because more than one input or an input and a previously nontraded final good can be opened up to international markets. The first scenario is associated with V. K. Ramaswami (1968), who set out, in a two-page note, an argument about the superiority of allowing imports of a scarce productive input as opposed to allowing exports of an abundant factor of production when a country could gain by either flow. In the second scenario, the issue is whether to allow trade in a specific input, or to allow trade in the final commodity produced with the help of such input. Again, either move would prove beneficial—the question is, which one is better than the other. As well, I consider the consequences in each of these settings of allowing mobility of *both* inputs (in the Ramaswami case) or of the final good as well as the specific input (in the second scenario).

4.1 Choice of Input Mobility

Some of the surprise engendered by Ramaswami's original contribution attached to the utter simplicity of his assumptions. Two economies share identical technologies for producing a single homogeneous commodity, the only commodity produced. The production function is convex, and countries differ in their relative endowments of the two productive factors, capital and labor, which are of identical quality in each country. Despite this similarity in technology and factor skills, endowment differences ensure that factor returns are not equalized in this two-factor, single-commodity setting. Assume that the home country has a relative abundance of capital, leading to a relatively low return to capital and a relatively high wage rate at home. Allowing for unimpeded factor mobility for both labor and capital would, of course, increase world efficiency, and both countries would enjoy gains. Instead, suppose the home country is "active" in the sense that it can allow some of its capital to flow abroad and earn the higher returns prevailing there, controlling this outflow by means of a tax on returns earned abroad. Alternatively, suppose the home country could hire foreign workers at their prevailing low wage rate. They could be allowed to work in the high-wage home country, but with a tax imposed so that the home country receives the wage differential and home firms pay the same wage to all workers, whether home residents or temporary immigrants. In each case, the home country would gain. If only one type of factor flow is allowed, would an optimal amount of capital export raise a greater amount of real income at home than an optimal tax on foreign labor inflow? This was the question that Ramaswami posed, and the answer he provided was surprising in being so unqualified:

> *Optimal labor inflows are superior to optimal capital exports for a relatively capital-abundant country.*

A production box diagram is well suited to illustrate Ramaswami's basic argument. The dimensions of the box in figure 4.1 indicate total world (two-country) supplies of capital and labor. Point E represents the endowment point for both countries, with the active home country's origin in the southwest corner of the box and the foreign country's origin in the northeast corner. Thus the home country is relatively capital abundant. The contract curve is the diagonal of the box, representing distributions for which factor prices would be equalized in these two countries that share the same technology. If labor cannot be relocated between countries but capital can, let point A denote the amount of capital exports (EA) that would maximize real national income at home. The rationale for stopping short of the point (on the contract curve) at which rates of return would be equalized in the two countries is familiar: Restrict sales in order to get better returns (on the capital sent abroad), even if it means foregoing a positive rental discrepancy on the next few units of capital that could be sent abroad. The gains to be achieved from this policy of optimal capital exports are to be compared with the gains possible if, instead of letting capital go abroad, workers can be brought in from abroad.

Ramaswami did not proceed by making a direct comparison between optimal capital exports and optimal labor inflows. Instead, he used a technique that both revealed the rationale for the comparison and provided an opportunity for further applications of the reasoning to new possibilities. Thus in figure 4.1 consider point B, lying on a ray from point A to 0^*. The allocation of resources between countries indicated by point B corresponds to a situation in which the home country first sends amount EA of its capital abroad, where it will be employed together with EB units of foreign labor, and then brings this capital back home *together with* foreign labor of amount EB. Since point B lies on ray $A0^*$, factor proportions abroad are not altered by this change of location and therefore factor prices abroad do not get

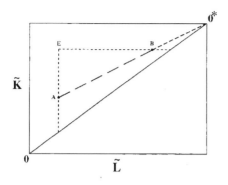

Figure 4.1
The Ramaswami setting.

changed. If, at home, quantity *EA* of capital and *EB* of foreign labor are sequestered, kept separate from the remaining bundle of factors used in production at home (represented by the vector *0A*), total world output and incomes received in each country would be identical to those in existence under the plan of allowing only capital exports of *EA*. Such a scenario would have the commodity produced at home with two different techniques. The convexity of technology, the bowed-in shape of isoquants, implies that the home country can do better by allowing the same technique for production to be used throughout the country—that is, the capital-labor ratio *0B*—instead of the two different techniques indicated by the slopes of *AB* and *0A*. Thus, argues Ramaswami, allowing foreign labor inflows of amount *EB* leads to greater welfare at home than can be obtained by optimal exports of capital of *EA*. The final stage in the proof follows from the observation that foreign labor inflows of *EB* might not be optimal—some other level of labor inflow could be even better, in which case the optimal flow must certainly be superior for the home country than allowing optimal capital exports and shutting the door on labor flows.

Suppose the optimal degree of labor inflow happened to be *EB*. This would lead to the same level of real income for all foreigners as the optimal export of capital—indeed, the same return to foreign capital and the same wage rate—and to a greater return to home national income (albeit the home wage rate is lower). Does this income gain really depend upon letting *EB* number of foreign workers into the country? Guillermo Calvo and Stan Wellisz (1983) have argued persuasively that it does not. Instead, suppose that home capital is sent abroad to work with foreign labor, but such capital is required to be used with labor in precisely the ratio in which it is used at home, perhaps by having such firms taxed by the home country for their use of foreign labor. This would, in effect, depress the foreign wage rate. A capital-labor ratio shown by the slope of a ray, *0B*, could be used both at home and in the foreign sector utilizing home capital. World output is the same as in the optimal situation, as is foreign income. The crucial point is that the same techniques are utilized for all units of home-owned capital.

In the Ramaswami setting two simple ways have been sketched for the home country to gain by introducing (impeded) factor mobility: Exporting capital or allowing inflows of foreign labor. What can be said for a policy of doing both? As analyzed in Ronald W. Jones, Isaias Coelho, and Stephen Easton (1986), such a combined policy does *not* improve the situation for the home country. Instead, home real incomes could be enhanced by encouraging a greater inflow of foreign labor, accompanied, as well, by an actual *inflow* of foreign capital, in proportions that would leave undisturbed the ratio of capital to labor still working abroad.[1] Better yet would be a policy that is initiated from original autarky point *E*. If both capital and labor are hired from abroad in proportions shown by the slope of *0*E,* foreign wages and rentals are undisturbed from their autarky values while the home country receives *all* the gains achievable by the increase in world production corresponding to the move toward the contract curve along ray *0*E*. This is what has been termed the "buyout" strategy, one that (unrealistically) leaves almost no productive activity abroad.

Contemplating a buyout strategy to obtain the use of productive factors from another country without disturbing their factor prices serves to reveal the potential inappropriateness of the simple assumptions of the Ramaswami model. Countries typically have productive factors that cannot be moved from one location to another—for example, land. In such a case, the attempt to withdraw other factors would have, as a general consequence, the effect of driving up the wages and rentals on these factors because their increasing relative scarcity abroad would tend to make them more productive there (Bond 1989; Jones and Easton 1989, 1990; Kuhn and Wooton 1987). A total buyout is therefore neither possible nor desirable from the home country's point of view. Nonetheless, the power of the convexity argument reveals that a "partial buyout" of the factors that are internationally mobile is often welfare enhancing for an active home country. Indeed, the argument even suggests that if technology abroad is somewhat superior to that at home, with this technology not embedded in the quality of productive factors, it may pay the (less advanced) home country to import a balanced set of inputs from abroad, paying the higher returns that they earn there—with world output *rising* as a consequence (Jones and Easton 1990). However, Ruffin (1984) illustrates how minor differences in a Cobb-Douglas production function can reverse the ranking so that

capital exports become the preferred strategy if foreign technology is (slightly) superior. In this case, any move in the
buyout direction would not enhance home or world
welfare.

Before leaving the Ramaswami model, one should note
the strong assumptions made about the wages that the
home country must pay to hire foreign workers. It may
seem unfair or infeasible to require foreign workers to receive (net) a wage that is less than that of their domestic colleagues (Bhagwati and Srinivasan 1983). Suppose, instead,
that the home country must pay prevailing home wages to
any workers hired from abroad but still retains the option of
controlling capital exports (and earning the foreign rate of
return on these exports). Its best policy then is to slam the
door on inflows of foreign labor (Jones, Coelho, and Easton
1986). Letting in foreign workers results in a lowering of the
rate of return that home capital located abroad can earn. The
Ramaswami ranking of choices of input mobility—namely,
labor inflows preferred to capital exports—would be
reversed.

Although the Ramaswami argument is based on an extremely simplified model setting, its relevance may become
more evident by considering the Calvo and Wellisz (1983)
scenario. One can find many examples of foreign investment by developed countries encouraged to exploit cheaper
labor markets abroad. In the Calvo-Wellisz setting, the
Ramaswami-type gains involved in letting the foreign abundant labor into the home market are obtained instead by
having home firms utilize techniques abroad that are similar
to those used at home. That is, foreign investors seem to ignore the cheaper foreign wage rate. This, in effect, suggests
the exercise of monopsony power whereby the demand for
foreign labor is (artificially) dampened in order to get better

terms of trade (lower foreign wages). In this setting, foreign countries might object to this practice. In a more realistic setting, foreign countries might welcome the use by foreign investors of modern capital-intensive techniques if it facilitates a transfer of technology.

4.2   Sequencing in the Move to Liberalization

Some sectors of the economy are often protected from the pressures of international competition, and such protection can be provided not only to the final product but also to inputs used in production. Services furnish prime examples, in the form of transportation, insurance, telecommunications, and banking. For example, a country's residents may be prohibited from holding bank accounts abroad and, at the same time, specific foreign inputs may also be prohibited from establishing businesses in the home country. That is, the right to do business abroad by local residents and the right of establishment by foreign firms might both be denied. If partial trade liberalization is to be considered, does it make a difference whether trade is to be allowed at the product level or the factor level? And, if completely free trade is the eventual objective, does the order in which it is undertaken matter?

To highlight the issues involved, I make some extreme assumptions in order to focus on the existence of a sector of the economy that is initially nontraded both in its output and in its inputs. I select the variant of the specific-factors model used in Jones and Ruane (1990). This is a highly stylized and simplified model. Suppose that the economy is capable of producing a number of commodities, each utilizing a factor specific to that sector in addition to labor drawn from a common national pool. The economy's endowment of labor and all specific factors is given. In the initial situation, *all* commodities except for commodity Y are traded on world markets at given world prices. Further, to enhance the degree of openness as well as the contrast between sector Y and other sectors of the economy, I assume that *all* specific factors except the one used in sector Y are internationally mobile, with returns determined by world market conditions. This casts the traded sectors of the economy into a Ricardian mode. In particular, with all the specific factors used in the traded sectors mobile internationally but with labor trapped within the economy, there will be, for this small open economy, only one tradeable activity that is selected for production: the one that maximizes the return (w) that labor would earn. Call this sector X. Thus:

$$w = \{p^*_X - a_{KX} r^*_X\} / a_{LX},\tag{4.1}$$

where the a_{iX} represent input-output coefficients for the specific factor and labor in sector X, and p^*_X and R^*_X are, respectively, the given world price for the favored commodity, X, and the world rate of return for the specific factor used in the X sector. Thus the economy earns income from several sources: (i) from labor, all employed either in sector X or in nontraded sector Y; (ii) from the amount of home-owned specific factors employed in the X and Y sectors; and (iii) from all the other specific factors that find employment in other countries as well as from any of the home-owned specific factor in the X-sector that is employed abroad. I assume that all this foreign-earned income is repatriated and spent at home. Local employment of the specific factor used in the X sector may include some foreign-owned factors, in which case their earnings are sent back to their respective countries.

The right-hand panel in figure 4.2 portrays the relationship between the relative price of the commodity produced in the nontraded Y sector and the return to the nontraded

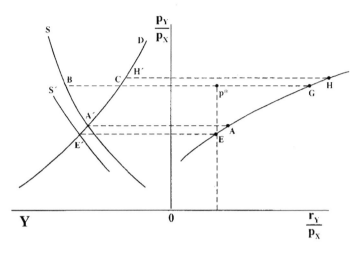

Figure 4.2
Goods trade vs. factor trade.

specific factor employed in this sector. The *magnification effect* illustrated in this diagram, whereby a given change in Y's relative price results in a greater-than-proportionate increase in the return to the specific factor used there, is not quite the same effect illustrated in the earlier discussion in chapter 2 (especially figure 2.3). With commodity X serving as numeraire in both instances, figure 2.3 showed an increase in the return to capital used in producing Y when its price rises and the wage rate falls. The reason the wage rate fell in figure 2.3 is that it was an illustration in the Heckscher-Ohlin context, in which an increase in the relative price of the capital-intensive commodity *lowers* the wage rate. Here the model is of the specific-factors variety. In this type of model, if labor is the mobile factor (as here assumed), its wage *increases* (somewhat) as the price of commodity Y increases. This would serve to reduce the magnification effect on the return to the specific factor relative to that found in the Heckscher-Ohlin model. However, in the current scenario, the wage rate is tied to productivity and prices in the X sector. Therefore, with the wage rate fixed, the magnification effect is somewhat greater, but still less than if the wage rate falls, as it does in the Heckscher-Ohlin case pictured in figure 2.3.

Home and foreign technologies are not assumed to be identical. Thus in the rest of the world the price-return combination for its Y^* sector, shown in the right-hand panel of figure 4.2 by p^*, does not lie on the technology curve appropriate for the home country. Indeed, as drawn, the home country is shown to have a technological comparative advantage in the production of Y (relative to X), in the sense described in chapter 2: The relative cost of producing Y at home would be lower if the same rate of return to specific factors were faced both at home and abroad (point E lies below p^*). Alternatively phrased, if the same relative price for Y were to prevail at home and in the world market, the home country could pay a higher return to the specific factor than it earns in world markets (point G lies to the right of p^* in figure 4.2).

Does this relative technological superiority in Y production imply that if the market in the home Y sector were liberalized in order to allow free trade in the product, the home country would export Y? Or, instead, if unfettered mobility for the specific factor used in the Y sector were possible, would the home country attract foreign supplies of such a factor to its own shores? Not necessarily. The pattern of trade or mobility that would emerge with liberalization depends upon the comparison between p^* and the initial equilibrium point for the home country, and this equilibrium depends upon the balance between local supply and demand in the market at home for nontraded good Y.

The left-hand panel in figure 4.2 is meant to display the equilibrium in the market for good Y at home. Assume that the initial equilibrium in this market is shown by point A' at the intersection of the supply and demand curves, thus also indicated by point A on the curve in the right-hand panel. The demand curve reflects not only taste patterns at home but also incomes earned by the endowments of all the national productive factors, whether employed at home or abroad. Given the wage rate, determined by the world price in the X market, the supply curve depends on local technology and the endowment of the specific factor used in the Y sector. I have assumed that the presumed technological comparative advantage the home country possesses in commodity Y (since p^* lies north of the home country's technology curve), as drawn, translates into a trade pattern in which the home country would export Y if trade in the product (only) were liberalized (because point A lies southwest of G in the right-hand panel) or, alternatively, translates into an inflow of the specific factor from abroad if such mobility were allowed but Y itself remained nontraded (since point A lies northeast of E).

How do these alternative trade patterns compare in terms of welfare gains to the local economy? Taking each of these scenarios in turn, suppose trade in the final product is allowed at given world prices. The home country would export commodity Y, with volume given by BC. The home country would also continue to produce commodity X, and the wage rate would remain unaltered. The big winner at home would be the specific factor in the Y sector, which would earn the higher return shown by point G. In the alternative scenario (no final goods trade but the specific factor becomes mobile), the specific factor at home loses, since its return falls from A to E with the inflow of this factor from abroad. Such an inflow shifts the supply curve in the left-hand panel to S' with the corresponding equilibrium at E'.

If the home country were to contemplate *partial* liberalization, with contact with the world market established at the final goods level *or* the specific-factors level, but not both, which option should it select? As drawn in figure 4.2, the option of liberalizing trade in the final product would yield larger gains since initial point A lies much closer to E than it does to point G. That is, the world relative price of Y is much larger than at home, while the return that the specific factor makes is only slightly higher than the cost of obtaining such a factor on world markets. Trade only in the service product would lead to exports of amount BC in the left-hand quadrant of figure 4.2, whereas the alternative of allowing an inflow of the specific factor brings about a shift in the supply curve from S to S'. This ranking of welfare outcomes would obviously be reversed if point A were to lie much closer to point G than to point E.

A more asymmetric set of possibilities emerges if the country's relative endowment of the specific factor used in the Y-sector is heavily skewed compared with the difference in technology between the home country and the rest of the world. For example, consider the initial configuration of service product price and return to the specific factor illustrated by point H in the right-hand quadrant of figure 4.2. (Such an equilibrium would necessitate drawing a new supply schedule in the left-hand quadrant, one that intersects the demand schedule at point H'.) In such a scenario, the service product is relatively expensive at home despite the home technological comparative advantage in its production. The reason lies in such a scarcity of the specific factor at home that its high return drives local costs above the world price level, p^*. Obviously if only one market is freed up, larger gains would be obtained by letting in foreign specific factors until point E is reached. An analogous asymmetric result would strongly favor trade only in the final product if the initial equilibrium were positioned southwest of E because of a superabundance locally of the specific factor employed in the Y sector.

So far comparisons have been made only between allowing trade in the service product, on the one hand, or trade in the service factor on the other. Suppose that the eventual position desired involves free trade in both (with labor the only immobile factor). If these moves are only to be implemented sequentially, another question arises: Will the first stage involve changing service output in a direction opposite to that required once completely free trade is allowed? That is, will a sequential move toward completely free trade (except for labor) require a reversal in the fortunes of the service sector?

Consider again the situation illustrated in figure 4.2. The diagram has been drawn to reveal that the country has a technological comparative advantage in the service sector compared with its best manufacturing alternative (sector X). Thus once completely free trade is opened up, the service sector will be the only active producing sector. The technology curve in the right-hand panel, drawn under the assumption that the wage rate is determined by conditions in the X industry, will shift up to pass through point p^* once the service sector can receive this higher price, with the wage rate driven up accordingly as production in sector X ceases. If the comparative technological superiority in producing services is greater than the effect of differences in factor endowments—in the sense that the initial equilibrium in figure 4.2 lies between points E and G (such as does point A)—the output of the service sector expands in the first step toward trade liberalization regardless of the sequence chosen (both points B and E' represent greater service output than does A').

By contrast, suppose that there is a severe shortage of the service-specific factor at home in autarky (so that point H represents the initial equilibrium). From point H, there are two possible sequences: Move first to G by opening up free trade in the service product, or move first to E by allowing mobility of the service factor. The latter involves a greater gain with partial liberalization than does the move to point G. Furthermore, and this is the point worth stressing here, the sequence of opening up the service factor to trade before the service product involves an expansion in the service product sector at each stage. The alternative sequence would require an initial *contraction* in the service product, to be followed by an expansion when completely free trade allows the service sector fully to commandeer the nation's labor force in the activity in which the economy has the greatest comparative advantage once all specific factors are paid their world return.

So far the normative conclusions have all suggested that a partial liberalization of trade enhances national welfare, regardless of the market chosen for exposure to world trade, and completely free trade improves national welfare even further. But what about internal income distribution, especially in regard to real wage rates? In the example illustrated in figure 4.2, the country has a technological comparative advantage in the service sector as opposed to the best manufacturing industry (X). Therefore, completely freeing up trade serves to raise the nominal wage rate. The price of services also rises to labor (as consumers), but the *real* wage must unambiguously increase unless initially the country had a severe overabundance of the specific factor used in services that brought about very low prices for services (a large distance southeast of E in figure 4.2). (In such a case, the cost-of-living increase of the move to free trade might harm the real wage.) However, if the initial equilibrium exhibits a lower price for the service product than in world markets (any point on the technology curve south of p^*), partial liberalization involving only the service product would harm real wages since nominal wages would still be guided by conditions in the manufacturing sector (X), and the cost of living for workers would rise. The only local gainer in such a situation would be the specific factor used in the service sector (as shown by point G).

4.3   Concluding Remarks

In this chapter, I have considered two examples that highlight the issue of choice in liberalization. In the first, the convexity of technology proved crucial in showing that a country may gain less by allowing its relatively abundant factor to seek employment opportunities abroad than by letting in some foreign supplies of its relatively scarce factor to work at home, assuming that factor were paid the lower return obtaining abroad. The benefits of this latter result could also be obtained for a capital-abundant country by having some of its capital located abroad but using techniques similar to the ones adopted in the high-wage home market instead of those more labor-intensive techniques used by the low-wage foreign country. The reason: This serves to inhibit demand for foreign labor, thus keeping its wage rate lower than would be the case if more labor-intensive methods were adopted by foreign investors.

The second kind of example turned attention to the possibility that initially restrictions were placed on the international mobility not only of an input but also of the output (in this case of a service sector). Once again, liberalization of trade for either entails gains to the country, but not of the same magnitude. However, now a different criterion arises as to which move brings the greater improvement in welfare: In which market is there a greater discrepancy between home price and world price? Such discrepancies appear both because technology is presumed to differ at home and abroad (with the home country arbitrarily having a comparative technological advantage in the service product relative to manufacturing) and because taste and endowment differences serve as well to determine initial prices in the two markets. These are features that are important in determining the output and income-distribution consequences of the order of liberalization if a move to free up trade in both markets is considered.

5   Produced Mobile Inputs: Middle Products

Tourists to Europe have often remarked that a cup of coffee costs quite a bit more in one country than another. Coffee is not grown in Europe, and it is unclear why the landed price of imported coffee beans should differ that much from country to country. Instead, the price discrepancy is usually attributed to country or local characteristics such as wage rates or rents—returns that differ among nationally immobile factors. In turning now to consider explicitly that internationally traded inputs are themselves produced, I emphasize that all final consumable items generally require two sets of factor inputs: internationally traded inputs and local inputs such as internationally immobile labor. Thus items that enter international trade represent both the *outputs* of some productive processes at home and the *inputs* into other sectors of home production. These traded items have therefore been labeled *middle products* by Sanyal and Jones (1982) in a model sketched out in this chapter. The basic idea is that international trade takes place in the middle of a country's productive spectrum.

5.1   A Two-Tier Approach: The General Framework

The role of international trade in the productive spectrum is illustrated in figure 5.1. The *Input Tier* of productive activity consists of a number of items (here just two, X_A and X_B) produced in a specific-factors framework, with given specific factors (V_A and V_B) used in two separate production processes in combination with labor (L_I). Quantities of X_A and X_B are middle products that enter international trade, and whose prices are assumed to be given for the small open economy. Labor and the specific factors used in the Input Tier are not traded, and their prices are determined in the national market. Trade allows the produced middle products from the Input Tier to be exchanged for a different bundle of middle products (perhaps a completely different set of products), a bundle that is more appropriate for production in the *Output Tier.*

Denote the aggregate value of production in the Input Tier by T_I, so that

$$T_I \equiv p_A X_A + p_B X_B. \tag{5.1}$$

If the trade account is in balance, which I assume is the case unless otherwise specified, the value of production from the Input Tier at world prices must equal the value of middle products used as inputs in the Output Tier, T_O:

$$T_O \equiv P_A A + p_B B. \tag{5.2}$$

Although figure 5.1 illustrates only two inputs available on world markets, there could be any number, including items not produced at home. These inputs are then combined with labor available in the Output Tier of the economy (L_O) in a specific-factors framework to produce consumption goods (here the two items, X_1 and X_2).

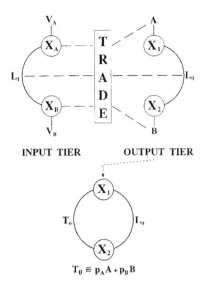

$$T_0 \equiv p_A A + p_B B$$

Figure 5.1
Middle products.

Note the role of international trade in converting a specific-factors framework into a Heckscher-Ohlin framework in the Output Tier. Although inputs A and B used in the Output Tier are specific in production (by assumption), their composition can be transformed by trade. What is relevant in the Output Tier is their total value, T_O. Thus in the Output Tier of the economy, two (or more) final nontraded consumer goods are produced with the aid of two factors, labor (L_O) and traded middle products (T_O).

The transformation schedules in the two tiers of the economy are illustrated in the two panels of figure 5.2. First consider the transformation schedule for the Input Tier, illustrated in panel b. It exhibits the bowed-out shape typical of the specific-factors structure wherein the underlying resource bundle consisting of V_A, V_B, and the quantity of

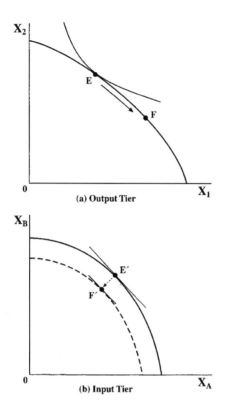

Figure 5.2
Transformation schedules.

labor assigned to the Input Tier, $L_{I'}$ are held constant. The movement from point E' on the outer transformation schedule to F' on the inner transformation schedule would be occasioned by a lowering of the quantity of labor assigned to the Input Tier with no change in the prices of traded middle products.

The transformation schedule in the Output Tier is shown in panel (a) of figure 5.2. This curve possesses the unique characteristic that *no* element of the resource base for activities in the Output Tier remains constant for movements along a given transformation schedule. Although the resource base is endogenous, the prices of traded middle products are assumed to remain unchanged for movements along a schedule. Consider a movement along the schedule from point E to point F. Such a move toward greater production of final commodity 1 leads the input bundle of specific factors to be rearranged by trade to allow the supply of A to increase and B to decrease. I have assumed that the first final commodity is labor intensive. By this, I mean that labor's distributive share in the production of the first final commodity exceeds such a share in the second commodity. This implies that from point E in panel (a) an attempt to increase production of the first commodity puts pressure on the labor market. In the typical Heckscher-Ohlin model with flexible technology, such a move would be accompanied by a reduction in the amount of labor required per unit output in each sector and an increase in the input-output coefficients for the other factor (which in this case is the specific factor used in each sector). This indeed takes place in the move from point E to point F. But this is not the end of the story. As the wage rate rises in the move from E to F, labor is released from the Input Tier. This leads to the move from point E' to point F' on the new transformation schedule in panel (b) and corresponds to an increase in the amount of labor available in the Output Tier, L_O.

With balanced trade, the reduced value of aggregate output in the Input Tier (from E' to F') is matched by an equivalent decrease in the aggregate value of traded middle products available as inputs in the Output Tier, T_O. In sum, the movement from point E to point F *along* the transformation schedule in the Output Tier is accompanied by an increase in the labor force allocated to that tier, a reduction in the overall value of traded middle product inputs, as well as an alteration in its composition favoring more A and less B. The slope of the transformation schedule indicates the relative price of the first commodity, which has been bid up by the increase in the wage rate. That is, the transformation schedule in the Output Tier is bowed out.[1]

If all inputs to the final production of consumer goods are endogenous along the transformation schedule in the Output Tier, what is being held constant? The prices of middle products are assumed to be given.[2] Furthermore, the total supply of labor (but not its allocation between tiers) is assumed fixed. Finally, the equality of the value of aggregate output from the Input Tier, T_I, with the aggregate value of inputs of A and B into the Output Tier, is maintained all along the curve.

All commodities produced in the Output Tier are nontraded. Therefore, if point E is the initial equilibrium point, a tangency exists there between an indifference curve and the transformation schedule, with the common slope indicating the relative price of the first nontraded consumption good. With all final goods in the Output Tier being nontraded, equilibrium requires an item-by-item equality between production and consumption.

5.2   A Simplified Two-Tier Approach

Many basic ideas of the middle-products scenario can be conveyed in a setting in which only one productive activity takes place in each tier of the economy. To highlight the role of international trade, assume the small open economy produces only commodity B in the Input Tier, because it has no specific factor V_A within its borders. It exchanges its entire output, X_B, at given world prices for amounts of A of equivalent value, where A and labor, L_O, combine to produce a single final consumer good, X_O. Equilibrium is portrayed in figure 5.3. The curve $0_I M$ shows diminishing returns to labor input, L_I, where the vertical axis shows the value of B produced (in A units) at given world prices for middle products. The other curve, $X_O X_O$, is an isoquant for the final consumer good, with inputs of A and L_O. (All production functions are assumed to be linear homogeneous so that the isoquant map is homothetic.) Point C, the equilibrium point, shows full employment of labor and balanced trade.

An algebraic sketch of this equilibrium, and the changes required in the wage rate to accommodate a deterioration in the terms of trade (i.e., an increase in p_A with p_B held constant) proceeds as follows. The full employment relationship is given in (5.3):

$$L_I + L_O = L. \tag{5.3}$$

Letting λ_{Li} denote the fraction of the economy's fixed labor force employed in the ith tier,

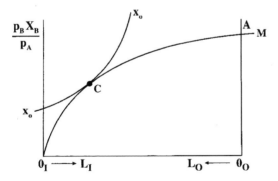

Figure 5.3
Middle-products equilibrium.

$$\lambda_{LI}\hat{L}_I + \lambda_{LO}\hat{L}_O = 0. \tag{5.4}$$

Now consider the breakdown of each of these relative changes. In the Input Tier, the demand for labor depends upon the technology and the wage rate expressed in units of the only item produced in the Input Tier. Letting γ_I denote the elasticity of the demand for labor schedule in the Input Tier (as revealed by the marginal product of labor there), its definition is shown in (5.5):

$$\hat{L}_I \equiv -\gamma_I(\hat{w} - \hat{p}_B). \tag{5.5}$$

The relative change in the quantity of labor used in the Output Tier depends upon changes in the input/output coefficient for labor, $\hat{a}_{LO}$, and the change in the level of output, $\hat{X}_O$, and is the sum of the two:

$$\hat{L}_O = \hat{a}_{LO} + \hat{X}_O. \tag{5.6}$$

Consider these in turn. The first term can be solved from the pair of relationships describing optimal input combinations by a tangency between the isoquant and a factor-price line (with slopes indicated by da_{AO}/da_{LO} and w/p_A, respectively), on the one hand, and the definition of the elasticity of substitution between the two inputs in the Output Tier, on the other:

$$\theta_{LO}\hat{a}_{LO} + \theta_{AO}\hat{a}_{AO} = 0 \tag{5.7}$$

$$-\hat{a}_{LO} + \hat{a}_{AO} \equiv \sigma_O(\hat{w} - \hat{p}_A).$$

Solving for $\hat{a}_{LO}$ yields:

$$\hat{a}_{LO} = -\theta_{AO}\sigma_O(\hat{w} - \hat{p}_A), \tag{5.8}$$

because the distributive shares, θ_{LO} and θ_{AO}, add to unity. Finally, changes in the consumption of the single item produced in the Output Tier must reflect the terms-of-trade effect of the rise in p_A. Because the term, θ_{AO}, also represents the fraction of national income devoted to imports,

$$\hat{X}_O = -\theta_{AO}\hat{p}_A. \tag{5.9}$$

That is, a deterioration in the terms of trade must cause final consumption to contract.

These various ingredients can all be combined in the full-employment equation of change, (5.4), to yield a solution for the terms-of-trade effect on the wage rate:

$$\hat{w} = \left\{\frac{\lambda_{LO}\theta_{AO}(\sigma_O - 1)}{\lambda_{LI}(\gamma_I) + \lambda_{LO}(\theta_{AO}\sigma_O)}\right\}\hat{p}_A \tag{5.10}$$

Two conclusions are particularly relevant in appraising the effect of a deterioration of the terms of trade on the nominal wage rate. First, any increase in the wage rate cannot, in relative terms, be as large as the price rise for imports. Second, the nominal wage rate may fall instead of rise, the outcome depending upon whether the elasticity of substitution between middle product A and labor falls short of or exceeds unity. If national (labor) and world (middle product A) inputs are highly substitutable for each other, the increase in p_A will translate into such heavier reliance on local labor that it must be drawn away from the Input Tier. If, instead, the elasticity of substitution were very low, labor would be pushed back into the Input Tier because of the loss of real income. The value of unity for σ_O is critical in the weighing of income and substitution effects. This can be seen in figure 5.3: The $O_I M$ curve would be shifted down proportionally when world p_A increases, leading to a lower isoquant. If σ_O were unity, the new tangency point would leave the labor allocation between tiers unaffected. The wage rate in nominal terms (i.e., relative to a fixed p_B) would remain the same.

What can be said about the *real* wage, the nominal wage rate deflated by the price of the single consumption good? It un- ambiguously falls: The final good's price change must be trapped between the two input price changes, and since p_A increases relative to the wage rate, so must p_O. The middle-products model thus leads to a strong outcome for terms-of-trade changes. With labor the only mobile national factor, its *real* return is hurt if the terms of trade turn against the country.

The outcome for the specific factor used in the B industry in the Input Tier depends upon what happens to the wage rate. If wages rise in nominal terms, the real return to this specific factor must fall. This would reflect an outcome not normally found in neoclassical competitive trade models: An external price shock that causes a loss of real income to the economy is shared by falls in the *real* income of both (all) factors of production. If the wage rate falls, the nominal return to the specific factor rises, but perhaps not as much as the price of consumer goods, depending upon the importance of the specific factor in the production of exportables. If this is small, and the nominal wage falls, the *real* return to the specific factor could rise, revealing (for the specific factor) "the importance of being unimportant."

This analysis of the effect of a deterioration in the terms of trade on the country's wage rate is useful in examining the importance of a real property of technology (namely, the elasticity of substitution between local and international inputs) in a comparison of the experience of two small countries, each with the same trading pattern and subject to the same external shock. (See Jones and Purvis 1983.) The great increase in energy prices in the 1970s serves as a useful example. Suppose two countries devote the same fraction of national income to imports of middle product A, whose price rises in world markets. The response of national wage rates could be substantially different—they could rise in the country with more flexible technology (σ_O high) and fall in the country with rather inflexible technology (σ_O less than unity). Jones and Purvis go on to show how the bilateral exchange rate between these two countries with a similar trading pattern could move in favor of the more flexible economy when both experience the same external shock in import price. That is, with appropriate monetary assumptions, the behavior of the exchange rate can be linked to real characteristics of technology.

Turn, now, to the impact of commercial policy on the internal distribution of income. Suppose a country levies a tariff on imports of A, with the world price unchanged if the country is small. What effect would such a move have on labor's income if initially there is free trade? The latter proviso ensures that a *small* tariff has no effect on the country's real income, and therefore no effect on X_O. The solution for the nominal wage change in (5.10) is altered—the numerator rising to $\lambda_{LO} \, \theta_{AO} \, \sigma_O$. However, the nominal wage still cannot rise as much as the domestic price of A, so once again the real wage falls. Does this imply that workers would oppose a tariff? Not necessarily, since labor is also affected by the redistribution of the tariff revenue. Given that the overall level of real income is unchanged and that the nominal return to the specific factor must fall (in contrast to the rise in nominal wages), the *real income* of workers would be improved for most distributions of the tariff revenue. Workers might applaud a policy move that makes the internationally available factor more expensive (because of the tariff), thus unleashing a substitution effect toward the nationally available mobile factor, labor.

Two "resource" constraints have characterized equilibrium. There is full employment of labor and there is balanced trade, implying that the value of production in the

Input Tier matches the value of middle-products inputs in the Output Tier. The importance of balanced trade can be illustrated by considering the adjustments required should a country attempt to run an export surplus. (This could be the outcome of a deliberate currency devaluation.) In figure 5.3, this would be illustrated by a parallel downward-shift in the $O_I M$ curve (not shown), so that a given positive discrepancy exists between the value of tradeables produced in the Input Tier (shown by the original $O_I M$ curve) and the value of tradeables available as inputs in the Output Tier (shown by an isoquant tangent to the downward-shifted $O_I M$ curve). Clearly, current consumption falls. The diagram can also be used to show that unless isoquants in the Output Tier are linear, nominal wages must fall. Although this serves as well to lower the price of nontradeable consumables, the *real* wage must fall. The attempt to run an export surplus pushes some labor back to the Input Tier. There is a clear redistribution of income away from mobile labor to the immobile factor in the Input Tier.

5.3 Many Activities in Each Tier

The simplification involved in allowing only a single productive activity in each tier of the economy serves to convey much, but not all, of the properties of the middle-products approach. The more general stance of allowing any number of productive activities in each tier, with no necessary balance in their numbers, requires little additional work and, in the Output Tier, reveals the importance of local taste patterns.

It is well understood that the specific-factors model generalizes in a straightforward fashion (Jones 1975). Thus in the Input Tier, suppose there are a number of productive activities, each requiring as inputs a type of labor mobile throughout the economy as well as an input used only in that particular activity. For given prices of middle products, any change in the wage rate will alter the Input Tier's demand for labor. This would now be expressed by an aggregate elasticity of labor demand, γ_I, a weighted average of such demand elasticities for each sector. The weights would represent the fractions of the labor force available to the Input Tier that are employed in each activity. And any increase in the quantity of labor utilized in the Input Tier would expand the transformation surface there in such a fashion that at constant middle-products prices all outputs in the Input Tier would expand and the wage rate would be driven down.

Earlier in this chapter, I described briefly the transformation schedule in the Output Tier. What was unusual about it was that the underlying resource bundle, A, B, and L_O, changed endogenously with movements along the schedule. Middle products A and B could be exchanged with trade so that a greater demand for the first consumer good, requiring A for its production, would be met by greater imports of A and smaller imports (or greater exports) of B. Furthermore, the amount of labor allocated to each tier is endogenously determined for movements along the transformation schedule: An increase in production of the labor-intensive final good would result in labor being released from the Input Tier to the Output Tier as the wage rate is driven up. The transformation curve is nonethe- less strictly bowed out as long as the ratio of labor utilized relative to the value of traded middle products differs between industries.

I retain the assumption that labor is the only nationally restricted mobile factor in the economy. In the Output Tier there can considered to be only one other input at given prices for middle products, namely, the aggregate value of traded middle products, since the composition of specific factors can be altered with trade. Therefore, if more than two final consumption goods are produced, the transformation surface becomes *ruled*. (The most simple example of a ruled transformation schedule when the number of inputs is smaller than the number of outputs is the Ricardian model.) What are the consequences? With more goods produced in the Output Tier than factors employed, either an indeterminacy in production takes place if the ratio of final goods prices is appropriate (i.e., the price plane is tangent to the surface along a rule), or for arbitrary final goods prices the economy would specialize to two (or one) final goods. Neither of these alternatives characterizes the situation in the Output Tier in the middle-products framework. The reason is that local demand conditions break any indeterminacy in production; if all goods are demanded, an indifference bowl will be tangent to the ruled surface in equilibrium. Furthermore, the oft-observed tendency of international trade to result in many more commodities consumed than produced is easily handled. There is no necessity for the number of goods consumed in the Output Tier to match up with the number of middle products produced in the Input Tier.

A technical problem plaguing much of standard trade theory in higher dimensions arises if all goods produced are facing given world prices and these determine factor prices with as many goods produced as the number of factors. The problem is that the matrix of input-output coefficients (or of distributive factor shares) must be inverted to go from goods prices to factor prices. The middle-products framework avoids this difficulty because production in the Input Tier is assumed to be reflected in the specific-factors framework. The items that enter trade are *inputs* into the determination of final nontraded consumption goods. For a small open economy, the only endogenously determined input price is that for labor, and the wage rate is determined in simple fashion, such as illustrated in figure 5.3.

So far, little has been said about the role of the composition of demand. Its importance can be revealed by considering the case in which two commodities are produced and consumed in the Output Tier. Although algebraic details are omitted here (albeit spelled out in Sanyal and Jones 1982), the role of demand can be revealed by considering two extreme cases for demand: Indifference curves for consumer goods are linear, on the one hand, or are right-angled (Leontief), on the other. In the latter case, the argument follows the lines of section 5.2, since it is as if a single commodity is being demanded (made up of the fixed proportions depicted in tastes). The former case is as if relative final goods prices are exogenous (given by tastes), and it leads to some interesting results. For example, suppose that the country levies a tariff on imports of commodity A produced in the Input Tier. What might one expect to be the fallout in income distribution? Would the wage rate rise if commodity A is produced with more labor-intensive techniques than any other activity (in the sense of highest distributive share for labor)? Not necessarily. With such flexible taste patterns dictating a fixed relative price for final consumer goods, the crucial question concerns factor proportions in the industry (X_1) in which A is an input. If this industry should be labor intensive compared with the other final good consumed and produced, the tariff-inspired increase in domestic p_A would squeeze that industry and cause the wage rate to fall. This is standard logic in the theory of effective protection.

Without going into the technical details, this case in which a tariff is levied on imports of a middle product usefully illustrates the role of the two extremes in taste patterns. Let σ_D represent the elasticity of substitution in demand (the relative change in proportion of final goods demanded along an indifference curve when their price ratio changes by 1%), and σ_S the analogous elasticity of supply along the transformation schedule in the Output Tier. The effect of a tariff on imports of middle product A on the nominal wage has been analyzed in the one-sector case, in section 5.2. The alternative extreme of linear indifference curves (σ_D is infinite) ensures that the relative price of final commodities does not change so that the wage rate falls if A is used in the labor-intensive final good. In the one-sector case, the nominal wage rises, and this is precisely the result that would obtain if two goods were consumed in fixed proportions (i.e., the case in which σ_D were zero). In the two-sector case in which indifference curves are linear, the nominal wage rate falls if the first final consumer good is labor intensive. For intermediate values of the demand elasticity, the effect of protection on the wage rate is a weighted average of these two extreme results. The appropriate weights are familiar from the theory of tax incidence and shifting: $(\sigma_S/(\sigma_S + \sigma_D))$ is the weight for the result of the case in which tastes are absolutely rigid and $(\sigma_D/(\sigma_S + \sigma_D))$ is the weight for the result of the case of linear indifference curves. Thus the nominal wage will be squeezed by the tariff if relative commodity prices for final consumer goods cannot change very much, whereas the wage will rise if tastes are rigid.

Finally, consider a change in middle-products prices originating in the rest of the world. Clearly, this country is made worse off if its terms of trade deteriorate and better off if, in-

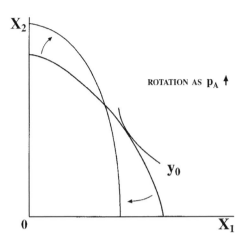

Figure 5.4
Transformation schedule rotation.

stead, the relative world price of the commodity exported
from the Input Tier has improved. This result is simply captured in figure 5.4. The increase in world p_A causes the transformation schedule in the Output Tier to twist in the
manner shown, assuming that at the point of intersection
the small open economy would be producing inputs A and
B precisely in the proportions required in the Output Tier, so
that there is no trade. Middle product A is imported for
higher values of X_1 and exported for lower values. The
transformation schedule in the Output Tier shows the menu
of possible consumption items, and this menu improves if
the world terms of trade move in favor of the country. What
is perhaps novel about the middle-products approach is that
the transformation schedule in the Output Tier is based on
an endogenous resource bundle, and its position is affected
by world prices of middle products.

One value of the middle-products approach for applications in macroeconomic analysis is revealed in situations in which the price of a middle product falls in world markets because of an improvement in the technology required in its production abroad. Suppose such a middle product is imported. Then in the relevant range the country's transformation schedule in the Output Tier is shifted outward, and the impact of such technical progress abroad would be captured in the aggregate value of *production* at home. If, instead, the imported item were a final consumer good, the home country's real income would indeed be improved (as its terms of trade change), but this would not be picked up in the value of national income produced.

5.4   Concluding Remarks

The middle-products approach is based in large part on the observation that almost all items of consumption require some locally provided inputs in addition to inputs available on world markets. This is clearly so if imported inputs are types of intermediate goods or raw materials or goods in process, and it is also the case if "merely" retailing activities are added to an imported or tradeable item that seems to be in final form (e.g., a foreign-produced automobile). (Such retailing activities often constitute more than 30% or so of the final price faced by consumers.) Thus treating all final consumables as nontraded is appealing. At the other end of the productive spectrum, it is natural to assume that all items that make their appearance on world markets require the inputs of some national factors of production. I have assumed here that the production processes involved are characterized by the specific-factors model in order to highlight the role played by a nationally mobile factor (labor) that is not produced and is restricted by national borders. The possibility of international trade is one that allows a country to alter the composition of middle products locally produced (in the Input Tier) from the composition of middle products used as inputs (in the Output Tier).

I have said little about the role of capital. Real capital movements, in the sense of shipments of machinery and capital goods from one country to another, can be treated as long-lived middle products. Perhaps of more interest is the existence of financial capital movements that allow discrepancies in the current account. In the middle-products framework, such imbalances are naturally treated as differences between the value of outputs of the Input Tier (T_I) and the value of inputs in the Output Tier (T_O). Thus a century ago, Great Britain could have T_O exceed T_I because of the return on capital investments abroad made in previous decades.

Throughout the analysis, I have focussed on the situation of a small open economy that is a price taker in world markets for middle products. As is by now standard procedure, this analysis could serve as a lead-in to the treatment of a large open economy, one that can affect world prices by its own policy changes. There is little in the middle-products approach that would require changes in the standard manner in which a country's reaction to an arbitrary change in world prices (of middle products) feeds into an explicit analysis of equilibrium changes in world prices.

In pursuing a set of normative questions in part II, I shall not insist on maintaining the middle-products approach. One of the characteristics of the field of international trade theory is that no single model is used throughout, with the choice of model (and simplifying assumptions) heavily dependent upon the nature of the questions being asked. For example, in chapter 6 I shall once again consider a locally produced commodity that can enter trade or be consumed directly at home without the addition of further inputs. This is merely a final consumer good in which the input share of traded middle products approaches unity. And in chapter 7, I shall consider the breakup or "fragmentation" of previously vertically integrated production processes. This serves to enlarge the set of middle products available on world markets. The role of service inputs, which in the middle-products framework adds value to traded goods in their transformation into final consumables, is, in chapter 7, to allow a fragmentation of production processes into separate segments.

Finally, the middle-products approach picks up a theme emphasized in earlier chapters. The number "two," so beloved in standard trade theory, emerges naturally in considering that products consumed require as inputs factors available only in national markets as well as factors available in the world market place. Some inputs are internationally traded and others are not.

II

Globalization,
Normative Aspects,
and the Changing
Role of Government

6   Normative Issues in Vertical Markets

Much of the normative discussion in the pure theory of international trade is conducted within the confines of a two-good model. This means that there is only one market, in which exportables are traded for importables. If a country has the ability to affect prices in world markets, and other countries are passive price takers, optimal strategy involves the imposition of an optimal import duty or export tax. The rationale is that such an artificial restriction on international trade will improve the *terms of trade*—the relative world price of the country's exportable will rise. This logic does not lead to ever higher rates of duty since the existence of the tariff or tax distortion introduces as well a *volume-of-trade* effect, whereby a reduction in the quantity of imports entails a loss because the world price at which they can be obtained falls short of their value at home (the domestic price). The upshot of the argument is that there is an *optimal* degree of import restriction, captured in the optimal tariff rate, the inverse of the excess of the foreign demand elasticity for imports over the value unity.[1]

International trade in inputs does not usually replace trade in outputs. Instead, the two markets coexist. This poses a challenge for trade theory, because it becomes necessary to investigate the nature of the link between markets. Taxing trade in an input into the production process disturbs the conditions of exchange in output markets and may well alter what is viewed as the optimal degree of interference in such markets. Early investigations of these relationships, dating back to Kemp (1966), Jones (1967), and Gehrels (1971), made use of the Heckscher-Ohlin production structure and the assumption of competitive markets in which commodity trade coexists with investment flows of *capital,* which can be used in either sector. More recent emphasis on markets that are imperfectly competitive shifted the focus to strategic behavior of firms that operate in world oligopoly or duopoly settings in which taxes or subsidies on inputs as well as outputs are important features of commercial policy. In what follows, I develop the argument in a core model that proves useful both for competitive settings, in which it is government strategy that is examined, and in imperfectly competitive settings in which firms make decisions in an input market in full awareness of the consequences in the output market in which they are active traders.

6.1   A Core Model for Normative Issues

It proves convenient to develop the core model in a specific-factors setting instead of the Heckscher-Ohlin context. Two commodities are traded between a pair of countries, and the *home* country not only exports one of the commodities but also exports an input that is specifically used to produce its export good.[2] To keep matters simple in this initial investigation, I ignore questions posed by the production of such an input and assume, instead, that it is available every period in fixed amounts. This fits the literature in the 1960s that investigated the optimal location in world markets of a fixed amount of homogeneous capital goods (but used in both sectors). The schematic "bubble" diagram, shown in figure 6.1, illustrates the home country producing two final goods, x_1 and x_2, with the use of labor inputs and two specific factors, z_1 and z_2. Exports of the first commodity from the home country are denoted by X_1, and shipments of the specific factor or input used in this industry are shown by Z_1. Domestic prices of x_1 and z_1 are given by p and r respectively (with freely traded commodity 2 serving as numeraire), and these will differ from world prices, p^* and r^*, if trade tax or subsidy wedges exist. Finally, let the home country's consumption bundle of the two commodities be denoted by (D_1, D_2).

The home country's budget constraint can be expressed in terms of domestic prices, in which case trade taxes and subsidies appear explicitly, or, more simply, in terms of world prices, as in (6.1):

$$p^*D_1 + D_2 = \{p^*x_1 + x_2\} + r^*Z_1. \tag{6.1}$$

Changes in *real national income* are defined as the *domestic* price-weighted sum of consumption changes and denoted by dy:

$$dy \equiv pdD_1 + dD_2. \tag{6.2}$$

Another useful aggregate measure is the domestic price-weighted sum of output changes. If there were no changes in shipments of the input, Z_1, such a sum would vanish for small changes in outputs, reflective of the tangency between a domestic price line and the transformation schedule. An outward flow of Z_1 would cause the transformation schedule to shrink in by an amount equal to the marginal product of input z_1, as captured by its price, r. Thus,

$$pdx_1 + dx_2 = -rdZ_1. \tag{6.3}$$

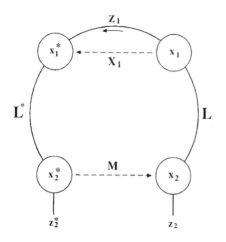

Figure 6.1
Home exports final good (X_1) and specific input (Z_1).

Differentiating the budget constraint in (6.1), making use of the two aggregate relationships, (6.2) and (6.3), reveals the *sources* of changes in real income:

$$dy = \{X_1 dp^* + Z_1 dr^*\} + \{(p^* - p)dX_1 + (r^* - r)dZ_1\}. \tag{6.4}$$

This relationship is basic in the analysis of the normative aspects of trade in outputs and an input. The first bracketed expression captures the *terms-of-trade* effects in exports of final commodity 1 and the input used specifically in its production. The second bracketed expression reveals the *volume-of-trade* effects in these two markets if there are any gaps between world prices (revealing what a country obtains by sales) and domestic prices (revealing what the items are worth at home). Such discrepancies can reflect either home-imposed taxes or subsidies or, in the case in which competition is less than perfect, the profit margins obtained by home firms in the two export markets.[3] Equation (6.4) suggests that any price change for an item entering trade and/or any volume change in exports of an item that has different prices at home and abroad affects national real income. Equation (6.4) reveals that the decomposition between terms-of-trade effects and volume-of-trade effects in the case of multiple markets is the same, regardless of whether the items entering trade are final commodities or inputs.[4]

Prices and trade volumes are not independent; foreign technology and demand conditions provide two links among these four variables. In competitive models of production, all input prices depend upon all output prices and the entire resource base of the economy. With commodity 2 chosen as numeraire, p^* and Z_1 are the only variable elements in foreign prices and endowments, so that the foreign return on sales of the middle product, Z_1, depends both upon this price and the quantity of Z_1:

$$r^* = r^*(p^*, Z_1) \tag{6.5}$$

Retaining the "hat" notation employed earlier, differentiation of (6.5) yields (6.6), linking the relative change in the price of the intermediate input to the change in the terms of trade and volume of input trade:

$$\hat{r}^* = \gamma^* \hat{p}^* - \delta^* \hat{Z}_1 \tag{6.6}$$

In this specific-factors framework, the elasticity, γ^*, is greater than unity; an increase in the world price of the first commodity has a magnified effect on the return to the specific factor used in that sector.[5] The second elasticity, δ^*, is positive, reflecting the fact that the home country exports the input and its increased availability abroad would drive down the input price as of given final commodity price. In what follows, I assume that δ^* is less than unity, as it must be if the international input flow is a small fraction of the foreign country's endowment.

The second relationship equates foreign demand for imports of final product 1, M^*, with home exports, X_1, and specifies that foreign import demand depends both upon foreign price, p^*, and the volume of its purchases of intermediate imports, Z_1. Thus,

$$X_1 = M^*(p^*, Z_1). \tag{6.7}$$

In differentiated form,

$$\hat{X}_1 = -\varepsilon^* \hat{p}^* + \{(Z_1/M^*) \, \partial M^*/\partial Z_1\}\hat{Z}_1. \tag{6.8}$$

The coefficient of the price change is the familiar elasticity of import demand along the foreign offer curve, drawn for a fixed amount of imports of the intermediate. The other coefficient indicates how a relative change in imports of the input alters the volume of foreign imports of the final good.

To continue with the development of equation (6.8), note that final goods imports represent the difference between demand and supply, making it necessary to analyze separately the terms $\partial D_1^*/\partial Z_1$ and $\partial x_1^*/\partial Z_1$. The former term picks up the positive income effect abroad of the fall in required r^* payments as Z_1 increases (driving down r^*) and equals (m_1^*/p^*) times $(\partial y^*/\partial Z_1)$, where m_1^* denotes the foreign marginal propensity to consume the first commodity, and $\partial y^*/\partial Z_1$, the terms-of-trade effect on foreign real income, is $r^*\delta^*$. At constant prices the output effect, $\partial x_1^*/\partial Z_1$, is positive. But more can be said. By the reciprocity theorem due to Samuelson (1953), this term is related to γ^* since the theorem requires that

$$\partial x_1^*/\partial Z_1 = \partial r^*/\partial p^*.$$

Assembling these components leads to (6.9) as the expression for the second coefficient in equation (6.8):

$$\{(Z_1/M^*)\partial M^*/\partial Z_1\} = \mu\{m_1^*\delta^* - \gamma^*\}. \tag{6.9}$$

The term, μ, reveals the relative importance of the two export markets for the home country because it is defined as r^*Z_1/p^*X_1.

The final decomposition of the change in home real incomes is obtained by substituting these components into expression (6.4):

$$dy = (\partial y/\partial p^*)dp^* + (\partial y/\partial Z_1)dZ_1. \tag{6.10}$$

where

$$\partial y/\partial p^* = X_1\{(1 + \mu\gamma^*) - [(p^* - p)/p^*]\epsilon^*\}$$

and

$$\partial y/\partial Z_1 = [1 - \{(p/p^*)m_1^* + m_2^*\}\delta^* - \{(p^* - p)/p^*\}\gamma^*]r^* - r.$$

If the home government can interfere in both markets, it chooses values of p^* and Z_1 that set each of these partial derivatives equal to zero. This it does indirectly by selecting optimal values for the tax or subsidy wedge in each market.

Let τ represent the ad valorem export tax rate on final commodity 1 and t denote the tax rate on sales of the intermediate input abroad so that

$$p^* = (1 + \tau)p \tag{6.11}$$

$$r = (1 - t)r^*. \tag{6.12}$$

Full optimization is attained when these tax rates are chosen so that the two partial derivatives in equation (6.10) are each set equal to zero. This yields as the optimal export tax formula for final goods:

$$\tau_{opt} = [1 + \mu\gamma^*] / \{\epsilon^* - [1 + \mu\gamma^*]\}. \tag{6.13}$$

If there had been no trade in intermediates, the traditional formula for the optimal tariff would be revealed in equation (6.13). When there is trade in intermediates, any alteration in the terms of trade for final goods would as well change the terms of trade on intermediate inputs for any given level of intermediate exports. And these two terms of trade are positively linked if the intermediate input is used in the production of the final export. The term, μ, reflects the importance of this indirect effect whereby a rise in p^* causes r^* to increase as well. Thus the optimal export tax rate is larger the more important is this indirect effect on the price of exports of the intermediate. This is captured in the downward sloping curve in figure 6.2.[6] The value, $\{1/\epsilon^* - 1)\}$, would be appropriate for the optimal tax rate on the commodity export if there were no trade in the input, which would be the case if the tax rate on input trade were sufficiently large. The lower such a tax rate, the greater would be the incentive to restrict trade in the final good because that serves as well the purpose of improving the terms of trade on the input.

Setting the value of $\partial y/\partial Z_1$ equal to zero in equation (6.10) leads to the optimal tax rate on earnings from sales of the intermediate assuming the final goods terms of trade do not change:

$$t_{opt} = \{(p/p^*)m_1^* + m_2^* \}\delta^* + \{(p^* - p)/p^*\}\gamma^*. \tag{6.14}$$

If there is no tax on final goods trade, the optimal tax on intermediate goods trade is δ^*, suggesting that as of given final goods price the rationale for restricting trade in intermediates is the standard one of getting a better price. This value is shown in figure 6.2 as the vertical intercept of the rising curve. This curve is rising because an export tax on final goods creates a gap between its foreign price and the lower domestic price (or cost). Therefore, restricting sales of the intermediate input has the additional benefit of forcing a greater dependence on final goods imports on the part of

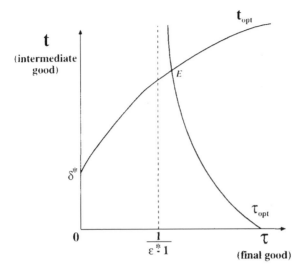

Figure 6.2
Export taxes on trade.

the foreign country, and these extra export sales create revenues for the public coffers at home. Full optimization by the home country, assuming no danger of foreign retaliation, is shown by point E. When a country exports an input that is specific in its use to its commodity export sector, the rationale for restricting commodity trade is enhanced in comparison with the standard result in which inputs are not traded. As well, if a country levies a tax on commodity exports, the optimal tax on exports of the specific input is larger than if there were free trade in commodities.

6.2 Relationships between Input and Output Markets

The core model imposed a number of assumptions. Among these was the assumption that the home country exports the input that is used to produce the final commodity that it also exports. This guarantees that the two export prices rise or fall together, and it encourages higher restrictions on goods trade as the intermediate export market becomes larger. However, the trade pattern might be different; the home country might import the commodity that uses the specific input that it is exporting. Such imports might be the consequence of previous years' exports of the intermediate that have encouraged greater foreign production of the final good. In any case, if the two terms of trade are inversely related, the possibility emerges that a country may wish to subsidize its final goods imports in order to get higher prices on its exports of the intermediate. The notion that trade flows might optimally be subsidized is usually considered to be a result associated with imperfectly competitive market settings. This case illustrates that competitive settings might also yield this outcome.

A further assumption made in the preceding section is that the home government has the option of setting trade taxes or subsidies in *both* markets. That is, it is able to optimize fully. Instead, trade agreements may inhibit the use of taxes in one market. For example, many countries have binding agreements not to raise tariffs on final goods imports (or tax exports) while reserving for themselves the right to control exports of an intermediate or raw material. This is a setting that brings to the forefront the relationship among markets. Restriction of input trade not only affects prices in that market but disturbs conditions in the final good's market as well, and these indirect effects must be weighed in determining what is optimal (in a second-best sense).

Suppose the home country's stance as an exporter of the first commodity reflects a production bias instead of a taste bias. That is, suppose the home country devotes a greater fraction of its national income to producing the first commodity than does the foreign country. As argued in chapter 3, this lends a presumption (through the hinterland effect) that a unit increase in intermediate input z_1^* abroad would raise its output of the first commodity by more than would a unit increase in z_1 at home. If so, a restriction on the exports of the input used to produce the first commodity would help lower world output of the exported commodity and thus raise p^*. That is, the argument in favor of the home country's restriction of Z_1 exports (so as to improve *its* terms of trade) becomes even stronger once account is taken of the indirect effect of improving the price of final goods exports from the home country. The rationale for this argument becomes even more persuasive if the scenario is altered to allow for a single large producer in the home export sector who controls both production of the final good *and* the specific input used in its production.

6.3 Vertical Integration and Imperfect Competition

Although the core model was developed in an explicitly competitive setting, it can be applied to a setting of imperfect competition. A scenario that captures the principle themes of the core model but shifts strategic decision making from the government to a private firm was developed in Spencer and Jones (1991, 1992). Let there be a single firm in the home country that determines the price of material input, Z_1, along with quantities of the final commodity, X_1 to send to the foreign country. A simplification is that the entire market for this final commodity is located abroad, although the foreign country also has a single firm producing for this market. The asymmetry between home and foreign firms is that supplies of the intermediate are more easily obtainable at home.[7]

To be more precise, I assume that the market in the first final commodity is characterized by duopoly between home and foreign firms, and that the home firm commits to a price, r^*, that it charges for the intermediate to the foreign firm. The home firm can obtain unlimited quantities of the intermediate at a lower cost, c, while in the foreign country there is a competitive fringe of suppliers that take price, r^*, as given. Furthermore, here I only investigate the Cournot setting for duopoly, in which each firm takes as given the output level of its rival in determining its own output. The key question for the home firm is its choice of intermediate price, r^*. Its decision making can be expressed in terms of terms-of-trade effects and volume-of-trade effects. For example, suppose the vertically integrated home firm is supplying some of the intermediate to the foreign firm and considers raising the price of this intermediate. In that market, it faces a positive terms-of-trade effect, but at the cost of a lower volume of trade in a market in which it is charging a higher price (r^*) than it costs to produce a unit (c). The spillover to the final goods market, however, yields both a positive terms-of-trade effect and a positive volume-of-trade effect; the increase in r^* causes the foreign reaction curve to shrink in and reduces the total supplies of the final good on the market, thus raising p^*. And, with foreign supplies reduced, foreign dependence on imports from the home firm is increased, and the home firm makes additional profits on those expanded export sales. This spill over effect on the final goods market is also referred to as the *strategic effect.*

In this setting, one decision faced by the home firm is whether or not to *foreclose* its export market in intermediates. By making the foreign firm rely exclusively on its own supplies of the intermediate product, the home firm enhances its position in the final goods market. However, such foreclosure denies to the home firm the profits that it can earn in the intermediate market. In the simple case in which profit margins are the same in the two markets and foreign supply of intermediates is completely inelastic, Spencer and Jones (1991) argue that vertical foreclosure is the optimal strategy but that the foreign country has the means to pry open the market for intermediate goods sales. The weapon? A foreign duty on imports of the final good would alter the profit margin comparison between markets and encourage the home firm to open up its sales of the intermediate abroad.[8] The rising curve in figure 6.2 serves to confirm this reasoning. Reinterpret the horizontal axis as the profit margin on the firm's exports of the final good, and the vertical axis as the profit margin on exports of the intermediate. The rising curve suggests that the higher the profit margin on final goods, the greater is the motivation for a vertically integrated export firm to raise its margin on intermediate sales (thus encouraging greater exports in the final goods market). Now play this in reverse. If the foreign country levies a tariff on home exports of the final good, the rationale for the home firm levying such a high price on intermediate exports gets weakened. Hence the foreign import tariff encourages the home firm to loosen up its restriction on exports of the intermediate.

There is another facet of foreign technology that bears upon the decision of the home firm as to what to charge for the intermediate. If the foreign supply elasticity for its own production of the intermediates is large, the home firm will be more tempted to charge a low price for intermediate exports. The rationale lies in the volume-of-trade effect of a reduction in this export price. There is a profit to be made in this market, and a lowering of the price faced by the foreign firm greatly expands the volume of exports if it drives out in significant measure the output of foreign firms generating their own supplies of intermediates.

What policy should the home government pursue in this case of Cournot duopoly competition between a vertically integrated home firm and its foreign rival? The question needs to be posed because the home firm need not rely on its government to affect prices; this it can do on its own. But the Cournot assumption that the home firm takes foreign output of the final good as given in making its own output decision provides an opening for the home government to tax or subsidize trade in a manner that credibly shifts the home country's reaction locus. To see what policy makes sense for the home government, recall the well-known result of James Brander and Barbara Spencer (1985) for this duopoly setting when there is no trade in intermediates. They developed an argument that an *export subsidy* would be optimal. Their reasoning is that such a subsidy to the home firm would encourage the foreign firm to reduce its output of the final good. Such an output reduction is not taken into account by the home firm, so that in its optimization calculation the firm overly restricts its own output. A government subsidy pushes the firm to a higher output level.

This widely cited result seems to stand on its head optimal commercial policy in a competitive setting—it becomes optimal to subsidize trade instead of to tax it. However, in my view it merely confirms the competitive result that restricted trade is optimal for a country that need not fear foreign reprisals. In the competitive case, home firms have no power over price and therefore no incentive to restrict output; the government must do it all via its taxation policy. By contrast, in the Cournot duopoly setting the home firm can restrict output, but indeed exceeds the optimal degree of output restriction since it does not take into account the foreign firm's reaction. Hence the government's optimal strategy is once again to achieve optimal restriction, but now this means a slight subsidy because the home firm has overshot the goal.

Once trade in the intermediate as well as the final good is allowed, it no longer always pays the home government to subsidize exports of the final commodity. The difference is that taxing such trade instead now causes a switch away from final exports toward greater exports of the intermediate. If the profit margin on intermediate exports is greater than on exports of the final commodity, such a switch is desirable. If there were no trade in intermediates this profitable alternative would not exist, so that a subsidy on final goods trade, the Brander and Spencer (1985) result, would follow. Trade in intermediates as well as final goods thus may alter optimal commercial policy.

6.4 Concluding Remarks

When a country engages in trade at both the output level and the input level, full optimization requires two instruments of taxation or subsidy. Figure 6.2 illustrates an equilibrium (E) with appropriate choice of two taxes, both positive. The possibility of optimally subsidizing a market could arise in a competitive setting if the two terms of trade, on the export of the final good and exports of the intermediate, move in opposite directions (which is *not* the case illustrated in figure 6.2). This could happen if the intermediate export is used specifically in the commodity that the country imports. (In the Heckscher-Ohlin scenario assumed in the earlier literature, such a conflict between terms of trade occurs if a country ships capital abroad and its own exports are labor-intensive.) In a noncompetitive setting a subsidy may prove optimal for a different reason: Although trade restriction is once again the optimal strategy, a firm might overshoot in its efforts to curtail output, so that the fine-tuning role of government involves an export subsidy.

In the analysis of vertically related markets, much depends upon the relationship between the two terms of trade. In competitive markets, prices are driven to the level of unit costs, so that the relationship between prices of inputs and outputs depends upon technological characteristics of factor intensities or factor specificities. Thus in the competitive specific-factors model, an increase in the price of the exportable final good is accompanied by an increase in the return to the specific input used in its production. And, in the absence of joint production, more can be said: The increase in the input price is a *magnified* version of an increase in the output price. It turns out that much the same can be said in the model of imperfect competition examined in the preceding section, but for completely different reasons. Output prices no longer reflect input costs, since the absence of free entry allows profits to be earned in output (and input) markets. However, market conditions do lead to a similar result. Consider a decision by the home duopolist to raise the price, r^*, charged the foreign firm for the intermediate input. This works like an upward shift in the foreign marginal cost curve (assumed horizontal since it is a price taker for inputs). If, as traditionally assumed, the demand curve facing the foreign firm (assuming a given home output) is flatter than the marginal revenue curve, the price of the final output would rise, but absolutely not as much as r^*. Furthermore, the Cournot equilibrium entails a rise in the output of the home firm, so that p^* rises even less. (Note that when r^* is raised, total world output is reduced so that p^* does rise.) Put in relative terms: Increases in r^* are associated with less than proportionate increases in final goods price, p^*. Once again, there is a magnification result.

In discussing possibilities for government policies in a globalized world in chapter 8, I return to the core model to consider the special case of a small open economy that has followed a protectionist policy concerning output trade, but allows unimpeded capital mobility internationally and is a price taker in the capital (or input) market. A strong result emerges. Without capital mobility, an increase in levels of protection harms real incomes. With capital mobility, an increase in levels of protection harms real incomes even more.

7   Fragmentation of Production Processes

In the scenarios of the preceding chapters, little has been said about the reasons why inputs into the production process become internationally mobile. Instead, I have concentrated on the consequences of input mobility, whether these inputs are themselves fixed in amount or produced by other inputs. Recent decades have witnessed more than just an increase in the volume of trade relative to incomes, since there has also been an increase in the fraction of such trade that takes the form of intermediate goods, raw materials, capital goods, or other middle products. Furthermore, production processes that have traditionally been vertically connected, so that all activity takes place in one location, are now frequently broken up or *fragmented* so that regions that are especially well suited to the production of parts of the process can now be utilized in producing these fragments.

Current examples of such fragmentation abound. The American automobile industry is one in which parts are produced globally, for example, in Canada, Latin America, and Japan for final assembly in the United States. (In a survey a few years ago, the *Wall Street Journal* found that Honda was the firm in the United States that used the highest proportion of local inputs). Leica relies on Spain,

Canada, and the Far East for its body and electrical parts, with only the lenses remaining in Germany. Computer companies such as Dell outsource many of their components, and clothing and footwear firms such as Nike rely almost entirely on foreign sources for production, retaining home inputs for design and coordination.

Such fragmentation is not without cost, and the framework put forth in Jones and Kierzkowski (1990), whereby *service links* must be established in order to connect widespread *production blocks,* is described in section 7.1. The importance of fragmentation in accounting for current changes in global trading patterns has also been the focus of more recent theoretical work, such as Sven Arndt (1996, 1997a, 1997b), Richard Harris (1993, 1995), Alan Deardorff (1997), Robert Feenstra (1998), Jones and Kierzkowski (1999, 2000), Gordon Hanson (1996), and Anthony Venables (1999). As well, conferences on fragmentation were arranged at Claremont in 1997, Burgenstock in 1998 (papers at the latter conference are collected in the volume edited by Arndt and Kierzkowski (2000)), and Hong Kong in 1999.

7.1 The Process of Fragmentation

Increasing returns to scale, especially the advantages of the division of labor, as promoted by Adam Smith, are key to explaining the process of fragmentation. As early as 1928, Allyn Young took up Smith's reasoning about the advantages of the division of labor in order to argue that "over a large part of the field of industry an increasingly intricate nexus of specialized undertakings has inserted itself between the producer of raw materials and the consumer of the final product" (538). To see what is entailed, consider the growth of a firm or industry. At initial stages all production may take place within a *production block,* in a manner captured by the traditional form of production functions relating inputs to outputs. Many of these inputs are obtained by purchases in outside markets, although some may be produced within the block. As output expands, it becomes feasible to consider a fragmentation of this process, with some components produced in the original location and others outsourced to different locations. At first, these locations may all be situated in nearby regions, within the same country. Such outsourcing has an attraction in lowering the marginal costs of production since advantage can be had in situating separate blocks in regions where intensively used factors may be more productive or available at lower costs. However, extra costs are created because *service links* are required to coordinate the outputs of these production blocks. The costs of service links include transportation expenses, costs of communication, and the costs of planning and coordination to match the quality and quantity of output flows.

Figure 7.1 illustrates how further expansions of output can lead to a greater degree of fragmentation, requiring ever more complicated service links. In figure 7.1, the total costs of various degrees of fragmentation (1,2,3) are illustrated, with each line reflecting an assumed constant marginal cost of production but with greater costs of service links shown by higher vertical intercepts for more fragmented production. Marginal costs are lowered by increases in the degree of fragmentation because a finer allocation can be made of inputs that may differ in price and productivity among regions. This diagram has been drawn to emphasize that the greatest source of *increasing returns* in production may come from the costs embodied in the service links. Costs of information, communication, and other aspects of coordinating production blocks are assumed to vary little with the scale

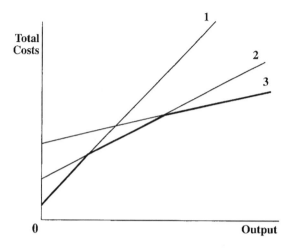

Figure 7.1
Fragmentation with output growth.

of production but to rise as the production process becomes more fragmented.

The significance of the growth of outputs and the breakup of vertically integrated production processes for international trade is that the process of fragmentation can spill over national boundaries. Two issues are involved. On the one hand, factor productivities and relative factor supplies (and factor prices) often differ more widely between countries than between regions of any single country. This would serve to promote fragmentation at the international level. On the other hand, it is to be expected that the costs of connecting service links would be higher if production blocks are located globally, and this would serve to inhibit such widespread outsourcing. As figure 7.1 suggests, growth in outputs can generally be expected to lead to increasing degrees of globalization in the fragmentation process because the relative fixed costs nature of service links can be spread more readily over larger output volumes.

One of the striking changes in technology in the past several decades has sometimes been referred to as the information and communications revolution.[1] For example, the costs of making a telephone call between New York and Los Angeles have been dramatically reduced. However, the relative extent of the cost reduction in telephone calls between New York and Paris has been even greater.[2] Computers have allowed virtually costless means of communication via e-mail and the Internet, with national boundaries no longer providing obstacles to such transmission. The use of fax machines has decreased the need for courier services and speeded up the communication of important documents. In addition, transport costs have been reduced. Companies have more widespread information about legal systems in other countries and are thus better prepared to deal at arms length with foreign providers of necessary components in case commitments are not honored.

In addition to changes in technology that have lowered the costs of service links is the change encouraged by growth itself. An increase in the number of competing firms in various countries has served both to lower costs and to reduce the risks that supplies from foreign sources cannot be made available on time. Accompanying these changes is the fact that many countries have proceeded to deregulate service activities such as insurance, banking, and transportation, and such moves, coupled with international agreements to lower barriers to trade, have all encouraged greater degrees of international fragmentation of production.

Technical progress that results in the reduction in the (mainly fixed) costs of service links among production blocks is rarely limited to one sector of the economy. In part, this is in the nature of service links—communication and transportation costs in particular. But the horizontal spread of fragmentation among industries can be stimulated in other ways (Jones and Kierzkowski 1999). Fragmentation of production blocks in many industries yields blocks that are more simple than entire vertically integrated processes, and such blocks may have strong similarities from sector to sector. The result: a stimulus to further technical change that makes these blocks from several industries even more similar, so that "one size fits all." Computer chips, once designed only for computers, have applications in cars, cameras, aircraft, and many other industries. Laser technology can be utilized in delicate eye surgery or in cutting textiles in a manner that minimizes waste. Earlier development of zippers, or the more recent discovery of velcro, have found numerous applications aside from holding together shoes or other items of clothing. These developments have helped reshape the industrial organization landscape. Industries may be sharply distinguished by the nature of the final commodity produced and yet share with other industries some of the ongoing advances in technology and make common use of new materials. The possibility of the application of some fragment or service link over a broad variety of industries serves as an important spur to the development of new technologies; research and development efforts are bound to be greater if the potential market in which profits can be earned is spread more widely.

These remarks serve to emphasize the two-way link between technological progress and fragmentation, whereby each encourages the other. As well there is the possibility that reductions in the costs of service links, eventuating in a further degree of outsourcing of activities, prompts a more rapid *adoption* of newly developed technologies. In most sectors of the economy, factors are somewhat reluctant to change the ways in which they are involved in the production process because that involves extra costs of learning and reductions in the rents associated with already acquired knowledge. As a consequence, firms may lag in their adoption of new technologies. However, a shock to the firm's activities, such as represented by a merger with another firm, may ease the transition to newer methods of production. Another such shock is represented by fragmentation. Separating out a production block and moving it to a new location may lower the costs of adopting the latest technology.

7.2   Some Consequences of Fragmentation

I turn now to consider some of the possible consequences following a reduction in the costs of service links. The focus is no longer on the increasing returns expected from a larger scale of production. Instead, I assume that a cost reduction in connecting service links has allowed for the first time an international fragmentation in a previously integrated industry. I concentrate on the consequences for a small trading economy, although such fragmentation is assumed to be widespread in the world economy for this particular industry.

Details are provided in figure 7.2, which focuses on the before-and-after situation in the affected sector of the economy, designated as industry 2. To simplify, I assume throughout that technology does not allow for input substitution, so that an initial vertically integrated production process exhibits Leontief-type fixed coefficients. For $1 worth of output at initial international prices, the isoquant has a corner at point 2. Two segments, *0a* and *0b*, are in-

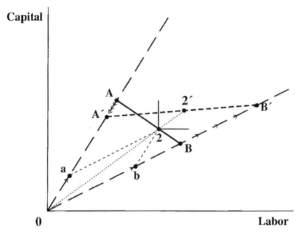

Figure 7.2
Price changes with fragmentation.

volved in the vertically integrated process that produces $1 worth of the second commodity. These segments cannot originally be traded on international markets, but the amounts of each required to produce $1 worth of outputs if priced at initial factor prices are shown by points A and B, with the slope of the connecting chord reflecting the factor-price ratio. As a consequence of the improvement (off-stage) in the costs of service links, it now becomes possible to engage in international exchange separately in the capital- and labor-intensive components. To keep matters simple, I assume that no extra costs are involved in assembling these components to obtain final commodity 2. (In reality, assembly operations are often outsourced to labor-abundant countries because these activities tend to be labor intensive.) Since the reduction in the costs of service links has been assumed to be worldwide, the greater degree of specialization now possible and the existence of different factor skills and productivities in various countries lead to price adjustments for the components.

The new international prices need bear no resemblance to the initial costs in this country (as reflected in points A and B for the two individual components). I have arbitrarily shown that the new international price for the labor-intensive component is lower than initial home costs, so that point B' now shows how much labor and capital are required to produce \$1 worth of this fragment. Technology in other countries may be superior to that at home for producing the labor-intensive segment, and fragmentation has allowed a finer division of labor and an opportunity for Ricardian differences in technology to be reflected in world production patterns and prices. By contrast, assume that this country happens to have relatively excellent technology for producing the capital-intensive component and that its world price now exceeds the initial prefragmentation cost at home so that less capital and labor are required to produce \$1 worth of the capital-intensive fragment (point A'). I have maintained the assumption that technology is inflexible, so that the readjustments to the new world trade situation leave factor proportions in each fragment unchanged. Although my assumptions as to the nature of price adjustments in each fragment are arbitrary, what is less so is figure 7.2's illustration that the cost of obtaining \$1 worth of the assembled commodity 2 has been lowered, by the fraction $22'/02$.

The concept of the Hicksian composite unit-value isoquant, often utilized in international trade theory, proves to be especially useful in tracing through the consequences of international fragmentation in the second industry on patterns of production, factor prices, and welfare in this small open economy. For a given set of world commodity prices, the Hicksian composite unit-value isoquant exhibits minimum bundles of factors required to earn $1 on world markets, with the composition of production changing along the isoquant. Thus figure 7.3 illustrates the initial situation in this country by the array of three fixed-coefficient isoquants for three different commodities that would, for each, represent the quantities that would earn exactly $1 at the initial set of world prices. The composite unit-value isoquant is the convex hull of these three isoquants, locus 321. In the postfragmentation situation, new prices are established in world markets for the capital- and labor-intensive components (as illustrated in figure 7.2), but to simplify matters I neglect any spillover effects to prices for other commodities. Thus the locus, $3A'1$, shows the new composite unit-value isoquant.

How this country is affected depends upon both its technology and factor skills compared with other countries (as depicted by the position of its separate unit-value isoquants for commodities 1 and 3 and the position of points A' and B') and its relative factor endowments, about which nothing so far has been said. Both the Ricardian emphasis on technology and the Heckscher-Ohlin emphasis on factor endowments are thus important ingredients in determining the consequences of fragmentation for the country illustrated in figure 7.3. If the country's endowment ray passes between points 1 and 2, the country initially produces these two commodities and as a consequence of fragmentation will lose the labor-intensive component of commodity 2 and instead produce just the capital-intensive fragment, A', along with the first commodity. A much more capital-abundant country would go from producing commodities 3 and 2 to producing 3 and the capital-intensive fragment A'. In the next sec-

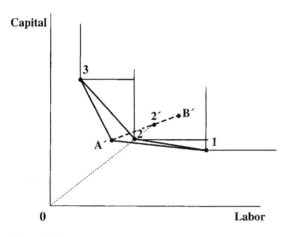

Figure 7.3
The composite unit-value isoquant—before and after fragmentation.

tion, I describe the consequences for internal income distribution. Here I just note the benefit that the country could expect from the new, better position of its composite unit-value isoquant and the reduced price that consumers would face in obtaining the second commodity.

Other possibilities could be shown. For example, the country's relative technology might have been superior for the labor-intensive fragment instead of the capital-intensive one, so that a new point B' could form part of the new composite isoquant, while point A' lies inside. Or the country might be able to produce *both* fragments at the new world prices. Of special interest is the diametrically opposite case illustrated in figure 7.4. As a consequence of fragmentation, prices have fallen sufficiently that *neither* fragment forms part of the new unit-value composite isoquant. This reveals that the original position in which the country produced vertically integrated commodity 2 was based not on a strong

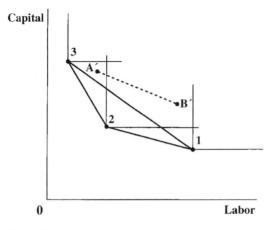

Figure 7.4
The loss of both fragments.

advantage in either fragment, relative to other countries, but on a lack of weakness in either fragment. By comparison, other countries that might have had superior technology in one fragment but could have been held back, in the cost competition, by weak productivity in the other fragment. An analogy could be found in the position of a class valedictorian whose top scholastic *average* across all classes masks a secondary performance in any individual course. Here a finer division of productive activities after fragmentation allows countries to uncouple relatively low productivity activities in order to free up fragments in which their performance is superior.

Although the postfragmentation composite unit-value isoquant in figure 7.4 is inferior to the original, it would be a mistake to conclude that this country has unambiguously been made worse off by the developments that led to fragmentation. The reason is that the world price facing consumers of an assembled unit of commodity 2 has been reduced, and if this commodity is a sufficiently large component in the budget, real incomes could rise.

7.3 Fragmentation and the Distribution of Income

Thus far, I have concentrated on the potential effects of fragmentation on the position of the unit-value isoquant and the nation's aggregate real income. More detailed investigation of the effect of fragmentation on the internal distribution of income between labor and capital (or unskilled labor and skilled labor, if the latter should be the interpretation of the "capital" label) requires specifying more precisely the country's factor endowment proportions.

Consider once again the situation depicted in figure 7.3, in which the country loses to foreign competition the labor-intensive fragment in the second industry. If the nation's endowment ray should reflect more capital abundance than required for the first industry, but less than required in the original vertically integrated second industry, the relative wage of labor must fall. That is, chord $A'1$ is flatter than chord 21. This is the result that many economists would lead us to expect: A country that loses its unskilled labor-intensive component of a production activity to the increased competition in world markets will witness a fall in real wages. (Alternatively, some would point to the present European situation where real wage declines are limited, but increases in unemployment result.)[3] Is this result a necessary concomitant of any type of fragmentation that results in a loss in the labor-intensive component? No. For suppose the country is more capital abundant, with an endowment ray exhibiting a higher capital-labor ratio than requirements in fragment A', but less than in the third industry. Relative and real wages *rise* in such a case. Such a result can be reconciled with Heckscher-Ohlin theory by using as an analogy a situation in which technical progress takes place but commodity prices remain constant. That is, in the first case (i.e., for a labor-abundant economy) fragmentation is like experiencing technical progress in the capital-intensive sector (at initial factor prices activity A' is superior to activity 2). By reasoning familiar from Heckscher-Ohlin theory and the Stolper-Samuelson theorem (Stolper and Samuelson 1941), such a change in technology aids capital (or skilled labor) while depressing wages. The second case (for a more capital-abundant country) reverses the scenario, with the original labor-intensive sector 2 being replaced by fragment A', an improvement at initial factor prices that eventuates in a rise in real and relative wage rates. And note that it is precisely in more capital-abundant countries that fears that trade and fragmentation will bring about a reduction in real wages are most frequently to be found.

This is a model in which factor prices adjust in order to maintain full employment, and thus it seems inappropriate as a setting in which to discuss aggregate unemployment. However, in the latter case discussed above, it is instructive to compare the total quantity of labor employed in fragmented (A') industry 2 with vertically integrated industry 2 before the loss of the labor-intensive segment. To facilitate such a comparison, draw a ray from the origin passing through the $3A'$ chord. Point A' receives a heavier weight on this chord than did the integrated activity 2 along the 32 chord before fragmentation. That is, more labor is employed in the capital-intensive fragment A' after fragmentation than was originally employed in the *entire* second industry. Fragmentation has allowed this country to jettison the part of the original activity 2 in which its productivity was relatively weak, thus emerging with an even bigger world market for the stronger fragment, A'.

Figure 7.3 indicates a possibility that seems to defy Heckscher-Ohlin logic. Consider an endowment ray flatter than $0A'$ but steeper than 02. Originally the economy produces commodities 2 and 3, and fragmentation is like technical progress in its labor-intensive industry (2). Nonetheless, there is a drastic *reduction* in the wage rate. The reason that standard Heckscher-Ohlin reasoning fails is that such logic is appropriate for relatively *small* changes, those that do not induce a change in the production pattern. But in this instance, the country not only loses labor-intensive fragment B', it is driven out of production of commodity 3, which is even more capital intensive than fragment A'. (Details are provided in Findlay and Jones 2000.) Compared with integrated activity 2 fragment A' represents a *labor-saving* improvement, and this factor bias suffices to reduce the real wage rate.

The purpose of these examples, and others that could be constructed, is not to discredit the *possibility* that the kind of fragmentation of production activities that is taking place in global markets may create downward pressure on unskilled wage rates in some advanced countries. Rather, they show how such a result, however plausible it sounds, is not a *necessary* consequence of fragmentation.

7.4   Concluding Remarks

This chapter has emphasized the important role of international *fragmentation* in previously vertically integrated production processes. The framework in which to analyze this phenomenon makes use of the concepts of production blocks and service links. Increasing returns of the type envisaged by Adam Smith can be obtained if various production blocks in the process are outsourced to regions in which the intensively used inputs are relatively inexpensive in comparison with their productivity. Such fragmentation is only made possible if the production blocks can be coordinated by service links consisting of transportation, communication, and financial activities. Service links are especially prone to exhibit increasing returns to greater volumes of output because they consist in large part in costs that are relatively invariant to scale of output. As a consequence, the greater costs of service links that are used to cross national borders can be offset by a lowering of marginal costs of production in the event that the scale of output is sufficiently increased. Such increases in scale of world output in a number of industries have fostered greater degrees of international fragmentation. This process has been aided by recent drastic falls in the costs of the service links that are required to connect various production blocks that are located in disparate regions or countries. Costs have fallen both because of some remarkable technological improvements in communication and because of a greater degree of deregulation of service activities, both nationally and internationally, all of which serve to foster greater competition. Thus fragmentation helps explain the greater extent of international input mobility that is the focus of this book.

International economic activity often takes place under the rubric of multinational corporations (Caves 1996). Is such a form of organization a necessary concomitant of greater international fragmentation of production? No. In enlarging the scope of their operations, multinationals may well outsource some fragments in arms-length transactions with foreign firms (e.g., see Hummels, Rapaport, and Yi

1998). Greater knowledge of foreign legal systems and the increase in the number of competing foreign firms willing to produce and supply various fragments can serve to lower any cost advantage to keeping production within the confines of a single firm. Offsetting this may be the importance to the firm of keeping new technology from spreading to potential rivals in an era in which technical progress is rapid.

It has long been argued that increasing returns and externalities help to account for the existence of *agglomeration* effects, whereby centers of economic activity are created, such as Silicon Valley, Hollywood, or the Rhur area in Europe (e.g., see Fujita, Krugman, and Venables 1999). The framework under discussion in this chapter suggests an alternative—namely, that increasing returns in the provision of service links can promote a *spread* of economic activity as the costs of communication are reduced. The rise of the software industry in Bangalore provides a good example. This sector often troubleshoots problems cropping up in activity in the United States and Europe. Given the difference in time zones it is especially useful, say, for businesses operating on Pacific Coast time to have solutions prepared overnight in time for the next day's activities. Although it is stretching things to imply that a new era of "cottage industries" will emerge, it nonetheless is the case that improvements in the costs of providing service links may counter some of the other forces that encourage agglomeration.

Finally, consider the importance of the process of international fragmentation for a number of countries that are characterized as underdeveloped or less developed. The theory of economic development has undergone much change since the important role of international connections has received its due. Export-led growth has been shown to surpass older varieties based on import-substitution strategies. The process of international fragmentation of economic activities has a potential for aiding development and growth. The possibility of establishing a production facility for just one small fragment in a less developed region exceeds that for capturing an entire vertically integrated process. Thus countries that admittedly do not possess a comparative advantage in service-sector activities might nonetheless gain by liberalization of trade in services.

Furthermore, it might be useful to distinguish two separate groups in such developing countries—the older generation and the younger generation. The older generation typically has more control over the *material* wealth of a country, and often the panoply of regulations and certain cultural aspects has been designed to protect that wealth from competing forces stemming from two possible sources: from foreigners operating abroad and from the younger generation. In many countries today, it is the younger generation that is more "plugged in" to recent technological developments, and members of this generation may have accumulated more *human* capital by receiving technical and business training in highly developed nations. Such contacts often make it easier for them to obtain financial credit and resources abroad in situations where local supplies and markets are deliberately more restricted. The older generation could be protecting vertically integrated activities that contain fragments in which local productivities are weak by world standards. The younger generation could be more receptive to fragments characterized by more modern technology. Firms in advanced countries wishing to establish production facilities in less developed areas will generally find more willing allies and agents among the younger generation. If the development process has been hindered by the array of regulations and norms protecting the older generation, the process of fragmentation and greater mobility of skilled personnel, technology, and capital exert pressure for change that surpasses that found in less globalized times.

8 Policy Options for National Governments

The literature on international economics is filled with discussions of policy options tempting national governments. What is the rationale for commercial policies, and what are their consequences for national income and its distribution? How should such a discussion be altered if explicit account is to be taken of the international factor movements and international trade in the inputs to the production process? That is the focus of this concluding chapter.

A basic point that needs to be stressed at the outset picks up a theme developed in chapter 2. The important role played by the doctrine of comparative advantage needs to be modified if there is any trade in inputs, and these modifications serve to highlight the importance of differences between countries in government attitudes toward regulation of business, provision of social overhead capital, and taxation. The idea of comparative advantage is linked to the notion that inputs are trapped by national boundaries, so that the only decision that needs to be made concerns the allocation *within* the country of these inputs. Ricardian theory stressed that a comparison of absolute productivities of such inputs between countries had no bearing on the allocation issue or on subsequent patterns of international trade. Instead, it was the *comparative* advantage of these inputs among sectors that mattered, and if a low general level of productivity did not alter the relative ranking among sectors, a country could still export commodities in which its inputs were less productive than in the importing countries. Government policies, such as taxation and regulation, might have equal incidence among sectors so that if no inputs have global markets such policies would not affect the pattern of trade. However, once any input has the choice of country location, a comparison of government policies has a first-order effect on which country will be able to attract that factor. Thus, a world in which some inputs are internationally mobile or tradeable is a world in which differences among countries in government policies have more of an influence on trade patterns than in standard treatments of trade based on comparative advantage. The doctrine of comparative advantage, with its emphasis on the question of what a factor *does* within the country, needs to share pride of place with the doctrine of absolute advantage guiding the question of where an internationally mobile factor *goes*.

The importance of national policies has another dimension. Government attitudes and regulations often have a direct bearing on which markets are allowed to be global and which are chosen to be purely national. In decades past, it was often argued that the rationale for market segmentation was to be found in high transport costs as well as international differences in language and culture. The stylized assumptions in trade models were that commodities could be traded, but (most) inputs and factors of production could not. The reasons cited for such asymmetries were frequently based on natural barriers (transport costs), different languages, and cultures. By contrast, in today's world governmental restrictions are frequently more important obstacles to trade than are natural barriers. Countries are in many ways like clubs of fairly like-minded people who wish to be guided by their own set of rules and regulations. Autarky vis-à-vis the rest of the world is not desirable, but neither is throwing open all markets, in goods, inputs, services, and factors, deemed attractive to most countries. The gains from being able to trade with other nations must be balanced by the loss of sovereignty or control over markets that this entails, and most countries choose to impose strict regulations on mobility of labor as well as on trade in some regulated services and on movements of capital.

The field of international trade theory is in large part concerned with the relationships between markets that are global and markets that are reserved for national agents (Jones 1995). However, even those markets that are closed to foreign competition are affected by productive activity that the economy pursues in world markets. Prices in national markets will increasingly be determined by prices in global markets. The central observation of much of trade theory, captured in some measure by the relationship between goods prices and factor returns, is that more active participation in production for global markets entails a *loss of control* over those markets that are purely national. This poses questions of choice for national governments.

One of the most widely cited contributions to international trade theory is the factor-price-equalization theorem, whereby countries that share a common technology and produce the same commodities (and a sufficient number of them) at common prices in world markets will find that their factor prices are brought to equality despite the fact that such factor markets are purely national. In my opinion, a more relevant theorem is that concerning *factor-price dependence,* which does not require any comparison between production patterns or technology among countries. Instead, it states that more active participation in world markets for some commodities lessens the degree of national control over prices in markets that are completely closed to alien agents. There emerges a conflict between potential gains from trade and a diminished degree of control over national markets. As a consequence, all countries shy some distance away from a free-trade stance for every good and factor. Furthermore, this connection among markets suggests why regional economic arrangements among a selected group of countries (which share some common national traits or objectives) may have more appeal than a universal lowering of trade barriers. Regional arrangements are often criticized for the distortionary effects that are thus introduced, without sufficient attention being paid to the fact that barriers to trade and factor movements among the nations in a regional block can voluntarily be reduced to lower levels than would be tolerated in wide multinational trade negotiations. This may especially be the case the more internationally mobile are inputs into the production process.

In what follows, I discuss three possible scenarios for the roles of national policies. The first is one in which governments have as their objective the maximization of the national welfare. Commercial policies are designed with that end in mind. Although some observers would consider that such an objective is realistically naïve for most countries, identifying those policies that do serve this purpose can prove useful in providing a benchmark with which to judge other policies. The second scenario is one that has received so much attention in political economy circles of late that I shall be brief in my remarks. Government is often persuaded to have its policies guided by the effects they have for particular interest groups. The third scenario will prove to be more controversial. It is one in which there is a kind of *civil war* being waged within countries, between the national government and the private sector. In each case, I will consider the consequences for national policy of the existence of significant international trade in inputs as well as outputs.

8.1   Government Policies for the National Interest

The terms-of-trade argument, whereby a large country could levy a tariff, quota, or export tax in order to obtain imports at lower relative prices, is still considered legitimate in suggesting a potentially effective way in which a large country might be able to exercise commercial policy to its national advantage. Of course it is subject to many caveats, the most important of which is the presumed failure of other countries to retaliate with restrictions of their own. It also needs to be reconsidered in the event that a country not only trades final products but also some inputs used in their production.

The discussion of normative issues in chapter 6 did focus on the effects of commercial policy on the national welfare and provided two alternative settings. The first of these involved purely competitive markets in which firms assumed prices were given so that they made no attempt to restrict output in order to get better prices. Instead, it was up to the government to improve the terms of trade by restrictive trade devices. When both an input and an output are exported, much depends upon the relationship between their prices. In the specific-factors setting in chapter 6 if the exported input is used in the country's exported commodity, improvements in one of the terms of trade spill over to cause improvements in the other, reenforcing the arguments for trade restriction. However, a subsidy on a country's goods exports, serving to raise the foreign relative price of that country's imports abroad, could be called for if the exported input is used in the production of the nation's imported commodity and if these exports are relatively large. Thus even in competitive settings, commercial policy guided by the national interest can lead to trade subsidies.

In the second setting, a vertically integrated firm exports a final product and is a dominant supplier (and exporter) of an intermediate to a single foreign firm with which it competes in the final goods market in Cournot fashion. If there were no trade in the intermediate, the Brander and Spencer (1985) result, whereby government policy at home calls for a subsidy on commodity exports, would emerge. The rationale is that although the home firm has the power and incentive to raise price by cutting back on output, this firm overshoots the nationally optimal level of restriction (since it ignores the foreign reduction in supply). The stage is then set for the government to correct matters in the national interest by providing a subsidy to exports. Although such a policy sounds diametrically opposite to the competitive result in which government taxes trade, it achieves the same objective (of optimal trade *restriction*). The difference is that such restriction is undertaken primarily by the firm instead of by the government. Commercial policy in the form of an export subsidy is required because the firm is guilty of restricting exports too much. If the firm also exports the intermediate, and if it earns a profit margin in this market that happens to exceed that in the final goods market, optimal policy for the government switches to one of taxing exports of the final good.

All this discussion presumes the country (or firm) is large. If a country is too small to affect its terms of trade, a policy of free trade is considered optimal for the national welfare. But suppose the country has nonetheless imposed a tariff on its imports. As well, suppose that real capital is internationally mobile, whether intersectorally mobile or specifically used in its export sector or import sector. Furthermore, suppose the country is too small to affect the world rate of return to such capital and that it imposes no restrictions on its international mobility. From an initial equilibrium, the commodity tariff is increased. If no *further* movement of real capital were allowed, the country would harm itself by the tariff increase. That is the standard result. If now capital is freed up to move, the country's real income falls by more. And this is a result that holds regardless of whether the capital is specific to the import-competing sector (in which case more capital flows in) or to the export sector (in which case capital gets repatriated). I consider first this specific-factors case and then the more subtle analysis appropriate to the Heckscher-Ohlin possibility that real capital is mobile between sectors.

To see how this general result can be obtained, reconsider the expression for real income changes shown in equation (6.4). Three of the four terms disappear since the small country cannot affect either of the terms of trade and it imposes no restrictions on the capital flow. To fit the current discussion, replace the change in exports, dX_1, with the change in imports, dM, with domestic price (call it p) higher than world price (p^*):

$$dy = (p - p^*)\, dM. \tag{8.1}$$

An increase in the preexisting tariff on final goods imports sends a signal to the domestic rate of return to capital. This

return will increase if capital is used in the import-competing sector, leading to a further capital inflow and a consequent reduction in imports as local import-competing
production expands. By contrast, the rate of return to any
specific capital used in the export sector would be driven
down by the tariff, inducing such capital to leave, thus cutting back on exports (and therefore imports). Once again the
term dM in (8.1) is negative, and the fall in income is enhanced by the induced capital flow. Equation (8.1) depicts
the *volume-of-trade* effect, whereby the reduction in imports
implies less is purchased in a market in which the country's
cost of obtaining goods is lower than its value at home.
(More details are provided in Jones (1984), Ohyama (1986),
and Neary and Ruane (1988)). Figure 8.1 illustrates that
from point A an increase in the tariff rate lowers real income
if capital is prevented from moving, and it will lower real
incomes by more if the capital flow is allowed to be
endogenous.

The classic result obtained by Mundell (1957) and discussed in chapter 1 comes to mind in considering the reper-
cussions of capital flows on trade volumes and welfare in
the Heckscher-Ohlin model. What Mundell demonstrated is
that if two-countries share the identical technology in a two-
factor setting, in which inputs are intersectorally mobile,
any tariff leads to an international flow of capital that serves
to nullify the effects of the tariff. National welfare and factor
prices remain what they were originally. However, suppose
that countries do *not* share the same technology, but that an
initial tariff rate inserts such a wedge between relative commodity prices in the two countries that rates of return to
capital are equalized with both goods being produced in
both economies. The tariff rate just matches the difference in
technologies between countries. Now let the tariff rate rise,

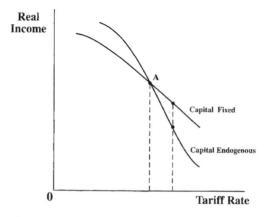

Figure 8.1
Small open economy with tariff.

say on imports of the home country's capital-intensive commodity. This causes the rate of return to capital at home to exceed its value abroad, with a subsequent inflow of capital that reduces the volume of imports. However, unlike the specific-factors setting, the capital flow does not affect rates of return in either country as long as trade in commodities still keeps relative commodity prices apart by the amount of the tariff. Eventually, the capital flow causes commodity trade to cease and continues until commodity prices reestablish their initial position at which rates of return are again equalized. But even a small tariff hike causes a finite change in real income because it completely wipes out trade. In the Mundell setting, there was no initial price discrepancy in equation (8.1) and therefore no welfare effects of the tariff.

Although this result is quite general in the setting described above, it can be overturned in the real world, primarily because of the standard treatment of taxes whereby the host country has first taxing claim on the income base earned by capital from the source country. As well, a country may deliberately use tariffs in order to attract capital (the "tariff-factory" argument) if it could thereby gain technical knowledge about new production processes or if its labor force could gain skills working with foreign capital in its import-competing sector.

8.2 National Policy and Special Interest Groups

National policies are not always driven by a concern for the overall national welfare. Today's thriving branch of political economy serves as a vivid reminder of the pressures of particular interest groups to have public policy harnessed to their own specific needs.[1] The theory of international trade is well suited to dealing with some of these issues because it has for long been concerned not only with the international distribution of real incomes, but also with the effects of government policies on the functional distribution of real income within a country.

It has been over half a century since the appearance of the article by Stolper and Samuelson (1941) concerning the possible effect of a nation's import duty on the real wage if the country is importing labor-intensive commodities. They argued that such a tariff would shift resources to the labor-intensive industry, thus increasing the ratio of other inputs (land, in their case) to labor and raising labor's marginal product in both sectors of the economy. Although much ink has since been spilled in the attempt either to generalize or to debunk this proposition, a quite important result can be stated for more general settings. Retain the Stolper-Samuelson framework of competitive markets in which technology is nonjoint (each activity combines factors to produce a single commodity). There are in principle two ways to provide public support for *any* selected factor in a manner that guarantees that its real income will increase. The first is the direct method of a grant or subsidy to the factor. Not the least of possible objections to this procedure as viewed by the factor is its obvious nature—such subsidies are usually transparent as a redistribution device. An alternative is for government to use its taxation or regulation policies, or alter its spending pattern, so as to change the array of relative commodity prices and, through such a policy, *indirectly* to alter factor returns. What extra conditions must be added to guarantee that this indirect method of changing commodity prices will suffice to improve the factor's real income? Only that there are a sufficient number of commodities produced—at least equal to the number of factors (Jones 1985). This is not to say that it would be easy to identify this required change in relative commodity prices, but it does establish the principle that the distribution of income can be affected in a powerful fashion by the indirect route of disturbing markets for commodities.

The Stolper-Samuelson proposition not only gave us an easy lower-dimensional example and demonstration of this proposition, but also revealed that the appropriate factor's return could be raised unambiguously *without* raiding government tax collections. Rent seeking in the form of attaching claims to government revenue may be prevalent in some countries, but the Stolper-Samuelson theorem showed how labor's real income could be advanced without considering any distribution of the tariff proceeds to private hands. One of the great achievements of the theory of international trade has been the analysis of functional income distribution in the context of simple general equilibrium models. The Stolper-Samuelson result is proven using the simplest

Heckscher-Ohlin model, but the specific-factors framework
reveals how the real returns to factors that are specifically
used in an occupation can also be unambiguously raised by
a simple increase in that industry's relative price. (The real
return to the mobile factor cannot be guaranteed such an increase.) Many government regulations and licensing proce-
dures serve to control entry into certain occupations, thus
providing the very conditions required for specific factors to
benefit from price changes. Specific factors are all about
rents, and government policies have the effect of redistribut-
ing such rents as well as controlling entry into specific industries or jobs.

Over thirty years ago, international trade economists
were concerned with an issue involving international trade
in inputs, commercial policy, and the internal distribution of
income. This was the question of which sector of the economy most would benefit from tariffs on trade imposed, not
only on imports of final commodities but also on imports of
intermediate goods required in local import-competing production. The concept introduced by W. Max Corden (1966)
and others was that of the *effective rate of protection*. The observation most frequently made was that a ranking of industries by the extent of tariff imposed on the final
commodity need bear little resemblance to the extent of protection effectively provided to domestic value-added in the
import-competing sectors. And such effective protection
could be much larger than suggested by the tariff schedule
for final consumer items if, as is often the case, tariff barriers
on imported intermediates and raw materials are lower
than taxes on final goods trade. The logic found in the theory of effective protection can easily be harnessed to show
how special interests can put a *spin* on the effects of commercial policy to argue that measures that are especially

helpful to them are really undertaken to benefit a broad, mobile factor such as labor. The specific-factors model is especially useful in explaining what might be termed "the importance of being unimportant."

I consider the argument in two stages. In the first stage, suppose an array of tariffs is imposed on both final commodities and inputs into their manufacture. Let each industry (j) in a small open (price-taking) economy use two (sets of) inputs—local domestic factors, considered as an aggregate, D_j, with return R_j, and imported intermediate products, I_j, whose price has been raised by a tariff on intermediates, t_{Ij}. The typical form of competitive profit equation of change for sector j is shown in (8.2):

$$\theta_{Dj}\hat{R}_j + \theta_{Ij}\hat{t}_{Ij} = \hat{t}_j. \tag{8.2}$$

From this relationship, it follows that the effective rate of protection provided domestic factors in the jth sector ($\hat{R}_j$) will exceed that indicated by the duty on the final product, $\hat{t}_j$, if (and only if) the tariff on inputs falls short of that on the final output. The second part of the argument proceeds in similar fashion to split up the gains from effective protection to the domestic value added in the jth sector into two components—the gains to labor, assumed mobile between sectors, and the returns to the factor of production specifically used in the jth sector (r_j). Thus,

$$\theta_{Lj}\hat{w} + \theta_{Sj}\hat{r}_j = \hat{R}_j. \tag{8.3}$$

Consider, now, the kind of argument for protection that could be used by the specific factor in an industry. Suppose that the alternatives are that the same degree of *effective protection* be granted one industry (say x_1) or another (say x_2). And suppose that the first industry is more labor intensive than the second (in the sense that θ_{L1} exceeds θ_{L2}). If these two industries are themselves relatively small compared with total activity in the economy, protection provided to just one industry or the other will have a minuscule effect on raising the wage rate. Note that the rate of return to the specific factor used in the labor-intensive first industry will rise by relatively more, if that industry is protected, than will the return to the specific factor used in the second (if that should be the sector that is instead provided the same degree of effective protection). However, the special interests in the first industry can claim they are more entitled to protection because theirs is the more labor-intensive sector. The "importance of being unimportant" in claiming special favors!

The greater current international mobility of factors and inputs introduces a new dimension to the use of government policies to affect the distribution of income. Some factors or businesses have the option of moving offshore if their national government pursues policies that attempt to redistribute income away from them. Laura Tyson, in her book *Who's Bashing Whom? Trade Conflict in High Technology Industries* (1992), discusses the policy followed by the government of the United States in the 1980s when it determined that Japanese producers of computer chips (in an age in which they had a decided advantage) were charging too *little* for their sales to American computer producers. The American government was persuaded to bring in antidumping charges, leading to a substantial increase in Japanese prices. As Tyson chronicles, this almost led to the departure from the country of national computer firms. More recently, German firms in 1999 agitated against government proposals to raise tax rates, threatening to leave the country in protest. Sweden is experiencing similar potential departures, adding to the losses already incurred by the flight of professional athletes to tax havens abroad.

The upshot of such mobility is the creation of two classes of agents: those who are internationally mobile, and those who are not. The interests of the latter are usually harmed by the departure of the former, and they often turn to national governments for relief. But just as the demand for government action increases, the potential supply of means to prevent such a departure may be limited. This leads to a third scenario—one that pits the public sector against the private sector.

8.3   The "Civil War" Scenario

There is no doubt that special interests in the private sector of the economy have a strong influence on the myriad dimensions of government policy. But in this third scenario, I focus on another possibility, not exclusive of such special interest motivation. I call this the "civil war" scenario, since it highlights a strong clash of interests between the public sector (government and bureaucracy) and the private sector of the economy. In this view, the government does indeed provide some public services such as maintaining law and order, including supplying sufficient military capability to deter aggression, and arranging some income transfers to form a kind of "social safety net." As well, there will be some parts of the private sector that are especially favored by government, a result, perhaps, of active lobbying efforts. However, in the present scenario an alternative view of government policies is contained in the assumption that the primary motivation of the public sector is to *regulate, monitor,* and *control* the activities of the private sector. By contrast, agents in the private sector are anxious to *avoid*, where possible, such elements of regulation. The main theme of this book is that greater international trade in inputs and international factor mobility demand new theory, both positive and normative. Such changes in the nature and extent of globalization involve new difficulties for national governments in their efforts to regulate, monitor, and control activities in the private sector. The reason: Agents in the private sector of the economy increasingly have the option of escaping these controls by fleeing the jurisdiction.

If groups in the private sector of the economy now find it easier to escape the efforts of their own government to tax, control, and monitor their activities, what might be the response of national public sectors to this increased degree of mobility? One possibility is to make arrangements with other public sectors (governments) whereby information is shared and attempts are made to realign the set of taxes and regulations so as to conform more closely with those in other regions that may be attracting agents in the private sector. One thing that a typical national government is not used to, and does not like, is *competition* from other governments for the services that it provides (and the taxes it collects). The word commonly heard when countries get together in regional arrangements such as the European Union is *harmonization* (of regulations and tax rates). But could another word for this be *collusion?* Or are governments really competing for footloose factors? There is no doubt that some competition exists—the appearance of tax havens in smaller jurisdictions (the Cayman Islands, Monaco, etc.) attests to that. Active competition among larger governments could lead to more uniform tax rates. But so could collusive arrangements. Much depends on the *level* of tax rates and the nature of regulation. In the late 1990s, much criticism

TRADITIONAL VIEW:

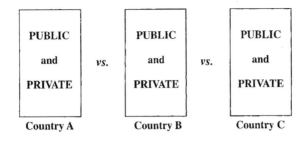

PUBLIC and PRIVATE	PUBLIC and PRIVATE	PUBLIC and PRIVATE
Country A	Country B	Country C

CIVIL WAR:

PUBLIC	- - - - -	PUBLIC	- - - - -	PUBLIC
— vs. —		— vs. —		— vs. —
PRIVATE	- - - - -	PRIVATE	- - - - -	PRIVATE
A		B		C

Figure 8.2
The "civil war" alignment.

came from countries like Germany about the low levels of corporate taxation in Ireland. Harmonization was the urgent message, but no suggestion was made that other members of the EU should *lower* their rates to the Irish level.

The "civil war" scenario is one in which governments are willing to forsake the standard notion (portrayed in the top row of figure 8.2) of joining with the private sector in order to pursue national interests that put them into conflict with other nations. As suggested in section 8.1, the standard analysis of commercial policy inquires about the means whereby a country can obtain better terms of trade. This could even lead to trade wars between countries. In the present scenario, governments are willing, instead, to sacrifice some sovereignty in order to join in agreements with other countries' public sectors (governments), thus enlarging the umbrella of their control over the foreign activities of agents in their private sector. This is what is shown schematically in the bottom row of figure 8.2. The diagram suggests that in today's global world, national governments may have more in common with each other than they do with their own private sectors. The agreements made among public sectors make it more difficult for agents in the private sector to shop around for the least-cost locale for doing business.

Some analogies can be found in the history of the United States stretching back to the 1930s. The depression era has in part been glorified in film and song by tales of bank robberies in which perpetrators were able to escape the jurisdiction of the state in which the crime took place. There was no necessity to create a new wider layer of government because it already was in existence. However, its powers to interfere with criminal activities involving several states were originally quite limited. The Federal Bureau of Investigation, although in its early days, was able to offer services to state agencies, for example, fingerprint identification. Some crimes were also made federal offenses, such as kidnapping. The attempts to extend voting rights in the 1960s led to aggravated instances of violence; murders took place in Southern states. But murder did not violate federal statutes, so that new laws were introduced. Murder victims were denied their civil rights, and that did become a federal matter. These examples, whereby state governments cede some of their authority to a federal government, prompted in some measure by the mobility of agents between states, find their reflection in the current international arena. The United States is active in cooperating with other governments in the crime area, especially in taking the initiative in drug enforcement. And little time passes before yet another announcement is made about agreements with other countries to share information on incomes earned by American citizens abroad, subject to tax at home. The recent Uruguay Round dealt with issues having to do with international labor standards and environmental concerns. If a forthcoming round of international trade talks sponsored by the World Trade Organization takes place, there promises to be attempts made to harmonize environmental standards and working conditions.

A counter to this scenario suggesting a more active role for government is found in the fact that some countries have denationalized their airlines, railroads, other transport activities, mining, and some of the roles traditionally reserved for the postal authorities. However, this may merely reflect a realization by government that its core competence lies not in production but in regulating and monitoring activity in the private sector. To the extent that national borders have become porous, those private agents that have been adversely affected in one country may seek alternative jurisdictions abroad that offer a more relaxed environment in terms of regulations and taxes. By joining regional associations, governments can in effect extend the domain of their control and deny their private agents access to better terms.

8.4   Concluding Remarks

The role of national governments is often portrayed as the design and execution of policies that further the interests of their citizens. In the standard versions of the theory of international trade, a sharp distinction was drawn between national markets for inputs and productive factors, on the one hand, and potential international markets for final commodities, on the other. The doctrine of comparative advantage supported the view that regardless of the level of national productivity, the possibility always exists of engaging in international trade in a manner that would ensure the country would gain. And the pattern of such trade could be relatively insensitive to overall national policies of regulation and taxation as long as these policies had a relatively uniform effect over sectors of the economy. This view has to be severely moderated once trade in inputs and international factor mobility are allowed, because a country's entire range of governmental policies, when compared with those of other countries, helps determine the direction of flow of mobile inputs. A country anxious to improve its terms of trade must take into account that such policy-induced changes in international prices serve as well to change the returns to internationally mobile inputs and factors. The possibility of using trade subsidies in some markets emerges, even if markets are strictly competitive. The portfolio of commercial policy instruments is further widened in the event that some international markets are dominated by a small number of firms so that profits are still earned in equilibrium.

The great expansion of interest in issues of political economy suggests that the motivation for government policy often is influenced by the lobbying efforts of special interest groups. There is no doubt that any exercise of commercial policy affects the functional distribution of income in addition to raising government revenue that itself may become the target of possible beneficiaries. Globalization and the increased degree of international mobility of inputs and factors have tended to create divisions within a nation between agents that are trapped by national boundaries and agents that are capable of relocating their activities abroad. Not all citizens have equal abilities to take advantage of foreign opportunities. To protect the interests of those agents and firms that feel trapped within a country's borders, national governments will be tempted by measures that add friction to international mobility. For example, in the Asian financial crisis of the late 1990s, some governments and economists became enamoured with the idea of taxing short-term capital movements. Part of the problem, of course, is that increased mobility of inputs tends to make supply elasticities higher. A disturbance to economies that alters their relative cost positions could more readily serve to encourage firms and even industries to shift the locale of their operations from one economy to another.

This is not a new phenomenon in principle, since it is often observed *within* nation states. For example, it is typically the case that communities centered on mining activities can be active for years and then become ghost towns when the activity becomes less attractive than in another area. In the United States, the Northeast used to play host to a thriving textile industry, but altered labor conditions and the introduction of cheap power in Southern states, allowing the use of air conditioning, did much to create abandoned mills and local unemployment in the North. The degree of factor mobility within a country is often greater than between countries, and the arrival of new activities will serve to contain individual losses to short time periods. Between countries such adjustments can be more difficult, and internationally immobile factors may increasingly demand that national governments do something to prevent such dislocations. Globalization and the increased mobility of productive inputs and factors pose serious challenges to the effectiveness of policies pursued by national governments in an attempt to aid special groups that are trapped by national boundaries.

This chapter ended, in section 8.3, with the "civil war" scenario that served to pit the public sector (government and bureaucracy) against the private sector (firms and individual agents) within a country. Although this can reflect only part of the truth, in its simplicity it does serve to highlight several features. It is supported by the notion that politicians are motivated by the desire to get reelected and bureaucrats are attracted by policies that will increase the demand for their services, such as having extra and more complicated sets of regulations. Furthermore, the private sector is the source of tax revenues, so it is natural that government will attempt to justify its expenditures that rely on these revenues. *National security* was often cited as a rationale for government activity. Perhaps in the present circumstances, this is often replaced by the promise that government can provide *personal security,* in the form of retirement benefits, health and education expenses, and compensation for unemployment and insurance against flood damage or other natural catastrophies. In any case, those private agents that have alternative options involving relocation in other countries may choose such a route if the burdens of government regulation and taxation seem less onerous abroad. In dealing with this increased ability of agents in the private sector to flee the jurisdiction, national governments may be anxious to make arrangements with other governments so that tax rates and regulations are brought closer together.

Whatever the motivation underlying public policies, it is clear that as national boundaries become more porous, the situation facing national governments must become more frustrating. Greater international mobility of factors for some agents and resulting increases in supply elasticities and location possibilities serve to make intercountry comparisons of public policies more relevant. This might lead to stiff international competition in the portfolio of taxes, regulations, and benefits offered to private agents. Instead, the forces of globalization may herald a more concerted attempt to harmonize the offerings and takings of public sectors in an attempt to limit the attractions of international mobility.

Notes

Chapter 1: Introduction

1. For a readable and nontechnical account of many of the issues involved in globalization, see Burtless et al. (1998).

2. For a thorough discussion of the literature that does consider factor mobility and trade in inputs, see Ruffin (1984), Svensson (1984), Ethier and Svensson (1986) and Wong (1995). Of course, the earlier literature on effective protection did consider different tariff rates on imports of intermediates and final commodities, and this topic will be discussed in chapter 8.

3. Marjit and Beladi (1998) have introduced yet another way in which factor mobility and trade can be complements. Immigrants to a country may bring with them a desire to keep consuming commodities (e.g., certain types of food) that in their native land were not exported. Their decision to import these goods expands the variety of items entering international trade. Feeney (1994) has argued that trade in commodities is a natural *complement* to financial capital markets in a risky world. The underlying rationale points out that financial capital mobility is a method by which countries can alleviate risk. Without these markets, the only way to reduce risk is to produce a more balanced selection of commodities and thus to forego some of the gains from specialization.

Chapter 2: An Internationally Mobile Productive Input

1. Earlier work allowing changes in the production of the mobile input in a Ricardian type of setting can be found in Sanyal (1983) as well as Jones (1980).

2. The following discussion is based on Jones (1980). See also Jones (1994).

3. This scenario is based on Jones and Ruffin (1975). A dynamic setting in which financial as well as real capital accumulation is allowed is pursued in Nishimura and Yano (1993). Another type of question, namely, the effect of factor endowment changes, either of the immobile or mobile factor, on trade flows is analyzed in Ohyama (1989).

4. With both capital and labor required to produce each commodity and with prices driven to the level of unit costs by competition, the relative price change for either commodity must be trapped between the relative changes in factor prices. In general $\hat{x}$ denotes dx/x

5. This is a movement along the Rybczynski line. See Rybczynski (1955). Along this locus, a country receiving capital (at unchanged prices) will witness a (linear) expansion of its capital-intensive commodity and reduction in production of its labor-intensive commodity.

Chapter 3:   The Hinterland Effect and Foreign Enclaves

1. Technically speaking, this is a four-factor, three-commodity model. Its structure also proves useful in asking about wage convergence between skilled and unskilled labor within a single country. Let this country produce an agricultural commodity (using land and unskilled labor), a standard manufactured commodity (using unskilled labor and physical capital), and a higher quality manufactured commodity for export (using physical capital and skilled labor). Such a 4×3 model allows an analysis of the differing fortunes of the two types of labor without sacrificing the usefulness in production of both land and capital (which would be required in lower dimensional models.) For details, see Jones and Marjit (2000).

2. Despite its relatively high dimensionality, this 5×4 model is amenable to simple analysis. With reference to the preceding note for the analogue to a model for a single economy, the scenario now allows land, two kinds of labor, and two kinds of capital (say, manufacturing capital and high-tech physical equipment used in an R & D sector).

Chapter 4:   Choice in Trade and Input Mobility

1. Suppose the initial situation is at point B, with an inflow of foreign labor of amount EB. Consider two alternatives: (1) letting a single unit of home capital to be relocated abroad, where its rate of return is higher than at home, or (2) letting a single unit of foreign capital into the home country,

hiring it at the foreign rate of return that exceeds the marginal product of capital at home. It can be shown that the *second* alternative is superior for the home country, since it serves to lower the wage rate abroad at which foreign labor is obtained. The first alternative raises such a wage rate. These terms of trade effects dominate the argument.

Chapter 5:   Produced Mobile Inputs: Middle Products

1. One could imagine a transformation schedule in the Output Tier (not drawn) which keeps the resource bundle frozen at values applicable at point E. Such a curve would be tangent at E to the schedule exhibited in panel a, but more bowed-in because the readjustments in the resource bundle are not allowed. The schedule drawn in panel a allows these readjustments, but since the wage rate is bid up in the movement from E to F, so also is the relative cost of producing the first commodity. That is, the schedule is steeper at F than at E.

2. Figure 5.4 will illustrate the consequences of a change in middle-product prices.

Chapter 6:   Normative Issues in Vertical Markets

1. The standard optimal tariff formula is derived in most trade textbooks, for example, in Caves, Frankel, and Jones (1999, pp. S-30, S-31).

2. A general treatment of the welfare effects of taxes on trade and investment in a framework utilizing duality techniques is found in Neary (1993).

3. With imperfect competition, the domestic price terms in the volume-of-trade effects should be replaced by average costs of producing the exported output and the input. (See Caves, Frankel, and Jones 1999, S-40–S-42). With this adjustment, the expression for changes in national income in equation (6.4) reflect the change in the exporting firm's profit. As suggested below, maximization of such profits is not the same as maximizing national income. Further details are found in Spencer and Jones (1991).

4. The case of multiple final products was discussed in Graaff (1949).

5. In a Heckscher-Ohlin setting, this elasticity would also exceed unity if in the foreign technology, the first commodity used input z_1 more intensively than did the second.

6. This diagram, and the accompanying analysis, is based on Jones (1998).

7. Indeed, the impetus for the papers by Spencer and Jones was provided by the decision in the United States to levy a 35 percent import duty on Canadian cedar shakes and shingles, primarily headed for the California housing market. Canada has more ample supplies of the raw cedar bolts and logs, and part of the American motivation lay in a desire to loosen up Canadian supplies of these logs.

8. With reference to the preceding note, American negotiators suggested that in 1987 the U.S. import duty of 35 percent on Canadian cedar shakes and shingles might be rescinded if the Canadians would loosen up their exports of the raw logs and bolts.

Chapter 7:   Fragmentation of Production Processes

1. The importance of major technological changes that affect a wide variety of industries is emphasized in Helpman (1998).

2. In 1927, a five-minute call from New York to London costs $75 (Pennar 1999, 37).

3. For an interesting analysis of the relations between European and American labor markets, see Davis (1998).

Chapter 8:   Policy Options for National Governments

1. For some major references, see Hillman (1989) and Grossman and Helpman (1994). The latter article lets government have both the national interest and special interests appear in its objective function.

References

Arndt, Sven. 1996. "International Sourcing and Factor Allocation in Preference Areas." Unpublished manuscript.

Arndt, Sven. 1997a. "Globalization and the Open Economy." *North-American Journal of Economics and Finance* 8, no. 1:71–79.

———. 1997b. "Globalization and the Gains from Trade." In K. Jaeger and K. J. Koch, eds., *Trade, Growth, and Economic Policy in Open Economies*. New York: Springer-Verlag.

Arndt, Sven, and Henryk Kierzkowski, eds. 2000. *Fragmentation:* New Production Patterns in the World Economy. New York: Oxford University Press.

Bhagwati, Jagdish, and T. N. Srinivasan. 1983. "On the Choice between Capital and Labour Mobility." *Journal of International Economics* 14:209–221.

Bond, Eric. 1989. "Optimal Policy towards International Factor Movements with a Country-Specific Factor." *European Economic Review* 33:1329–1344.

Brander, James, and Barbara Spencer. 1985. "Export Subsidies and International Market Share Rivalry." *Journal of International Economics* 18:83–100.

Burtless, Gary, Robert Lawrence, Robert Litan, and Robert Shapiro. 1998. *Globaphobia: Confronting Fears about Open Trade.* Washington, D.C.: Brookings.

Calvo, Guillermo, and Stan Wellisz. 1983. "International Factor Mobility and National Advantage." *Journal of International Economics* 14:103–114.

Caves, Richard E. 1996. *Multinational Enterprise and Economic Analysis,* 2d ed. Cambridge: Cambridge University Press.

Caves, Richard E., Jeffrey A. Frankel, and Ronald W. Jones. 1999. *World Trade and Payments: An Introduction,* 8th ed. Reading, Mass.: Addison Wesley.

Chipman, John. 1971. "International Trade with Capital Mobility: A Substitution Theorem." In Jagdish Bhagwati, Ronald W. Jones, Robert Mundell, and Jaroslav Vanek, eds., *Trade, Balance of Payments, and Growth* (Amsterdam: North-Holland), 201–237.

Corden, W. Max. 1966. "The Structure of a Tariff System and the Effective Protection Rate." *Journal of Political Economy* 74:221–237.

Davis, Donald R. 1998. "Does European Unemployment Prop Up American Wages? National Labor Markets and Global Trade." *American Economic Review* (June):478–494.

Deardorff, Alan. 1997. "Fragmentation in Simple Trade Models." Unpublished manuscript.

Dixit, Avinash, and Joseph Stiglitz. 1977. "Monopolistic Competition and Optimum Product Diversity." *American Economic Review* 67:297–308.

Ethier, Wilfred, and Lars Svensson. 1986. "The Theorems of International Trade with Factor Mobility." *Journal of International Economics* 20:21–42.

Feeney, JoAnne. (1994). "Goods and Asset Market Interdependence in a Risky World." *International Economic Review* 35:551–563.

Feenstra, Robert. 1998. "Integration of Trade and Disintegration of Production in the Global Economy." *Journal of Economic Perspectives* 12:31–50.

Findlay, Ronald. 1995. *Factor Proportions, Trade, and Growth.* Cambridge, Mass.: The MIT Press.

Findlay, Ronald, and Ronald W. Jones. 2000. "Factor Bias and Technical Progress." *Economics Letters.* Forthcoming.

Fujita, Masahisa, Paul Krugman, and Anthony Venables. 1999. *The Spatial Economy: Cities, Regions, and International Trade.* Cambridge, Mass.: The MIT Press.

Gehrels, Franz. 1971. "Optimal Restrictions on Foreign Trade and Investment." *American Economic Review* (March):147–159.

Graaff, Jan de V. 1949. "On Optimum Tariff Structures." *Review of Economic Studies* 17:47–59.

Grossman, Gene, and Elhanan Helpman. 1994. "Protection for Sale." *American Economic Review* 84:833–50.

Haberler, Gottfried. 1936. *The Theory of International Trade.* London: Wm. Hodge & Co.

Hanson, Gordon. 1996. "Localization Economies, Vertical Organization, and Trade." *American Economic Review* 86 (December): 1266–1278.

Harris, Richard G. 1993. "Globalization, Trade and Income." *Canadian Journal of Economics* 26 (November): 755–776.

———. (1995). "Trade and Communications Costs." *Canadian Journal of Economics* 28 (Special Issue, November): S46–S75.

Heckscher, Eli. 1919. "The Effect of Foreign Trade on the Distribution of Income." *Ekonomisk Tidskrift,* 497–512; translated in Harry Flam and M. June Flanders, *Heckscher-Ohlin Trade Theory* (Cambridge, Mass.: The MIT Press, 1991).

Helpman, Elhanan, ed. 1998. *General Purpose Technologies and Economic Growth.* Cambridge, Mass.: The MIT Press.

Hillman, Arye. 1989. *The Political Economy of Protection.* Chur: Harwood Academic Publishers.

Hummels, David, Dana Rapaport, and Kei-Mu Yi. 1998. "Vertical Specialization and the Changing Nature of World Trade." *Federal Reserve Bank of New York Economic Policy Review* 4 (June):79–99.

Jones, Ronald W. 1965. "The Structure of Simple General Equilibrium Models." *Journal of Political Economy* (December): 557–572.

———. 1967. "International Capital Movements and the Theory of Tariffs and Trade." *Quarterly Journal of Economics* (February):1–38; reprinted with pp. 31–34 deleted in Ronald W. Jones, *International Trade: Essays in Theory* (Amsterdam: North-Holland, 1979).

———. 1970. "The Role of Technology in the Theory of International Trade." In Ray Vernon, ed., *The Technology Factor in International Trade* (Washington, D.C.: National Bureau of Economic Research), 73–92; reprinted in Ronald W. Jones, *International Trade: Essays in Theory* (Amsterdam: North-Holland, 1979).

———. 1971. "A Three-Factor Model in Theory, Trade, and History." In Jagdish Bhagwati, Ronald W. Jones, Robert Mundell, and Jaroslav Vanek, eds., *Trade, Balance of Payments, and Growth: Essays in Honor of Charles P. Kindleberger* (Amsterdam: North-Holland), 3–21.

———. 1975. "Income Distribution and Effective Protection in a Multi-Commodity Trade Model." *Journal of Economic Theory* 11 (August): 1–15.

———. 1980. "Comparative and Absolute Advantage." *The Swiss Journal of Economics and Statistics* 116, no. 3:235–260.

———. 1984. "Protection and the Harmful Effects of Endogenous Capital Flows." *Economics Letters* 15:325–330.

———. 1985. "Relative Prices and Real Factor Rewards: A Re-interpretation." *Economic Letters* 19:47–49.

———. 1987. "Tax Wedges and Mobile Capital." *Scandinavian Journal of Economics* 89, no. 3:335–346.

———. 1989. "Co-movements in Relative Commodity Prices and International Capital Flows: A Simple Model." *Economic Inquiry* (January):131–141.

———. 1994. "Trade with Capital Mobility: A Ricardian Approach." *Nagasaki Prefectural University Review* (October):77–89.

———. 1995. "The Discipline of International Trade." *The Swiss Journal of Economics and Statistics* 131, no. 3:273–288.

———. 1998. "Vertical Markets in International Trade." In D. Pick, J. Kinsey, D. Henderson, and I. Sheldon, eds., *Global Markets for Processed Foods: Theoretical and Practical Issues* (Boulder: Westview Press), 161–180.

Jones, Ronald W., and Fumio Dei. 1983. "International Trade and Foreign Investment: A Simple Model." *Economic Inquiry* 21 (October):449–464.

Jones, Ronald W., and Stephen Easton. 1989. "Perspectives on 'Buy-Outs' and the Ramaswami Effect." *Journal of International Economics* (November):363–371.

———. 1990. "Foreign Investment and Migration: Analytics and Extensions of the Basic Model." *Keio Economic Studies* 27, no. 1:1–20.

Jones, Ronald W., and Henryk Kierzkowski. 1986. "Neighborhood Production Structures with an Application to the Theory of International Trade." *Oxford Economic Papers* 38:59–76.

———. 1990. "The Role of Services in Production and International Trade: A Theoretical Framework." In R. Jones and A. Krueger, eds., *The Political Economy of International Trade* (Oxford: Basil Blackwell), 31–48.

———. 1999. "Horizontal Aspects of Vertical Fragmentation." Unpublished.

———. 2000. "Globalization and the Consequences of International Fragmentation." In R. Dornbusch, G. Calvo, and M. Obstfeld, eds., *Money, Fac-*

tor Mobility, and Trade: The Festschrift in Honor of Robert A. Mundell (Cambridge, Mass.: The MIT Press). Forthcoming.

Jones, Ronald W., and Sugata Marjit. 1995. "Labour-Market Aspects of Enclave-Led Growth." *Canadian Journal of Economics* (November):S76–S93.

———. 2000. "Economic Development, Trade and Wages." Unpublished.

Jones, Ronald W., and J. Peter Neary. 1984. "The Positive Theory of International Trade." In R. Jones and Peter Kenen, eds, *Handbook of International Economics,* vol. 1 (Amsterdam: North-Holland), 1–62.

Jones, Ronald W., and Douglas Purvis. 1983. "International Differences in Response to Common External Shocks: The Role of Purchasing Power Parity." In Emil Classen and Pascal Salin, eds., *Recent Issues in the Theory of Flexible Exchange Rates* (Amsterdam: North-Holland), 33–55.

Jones, Ronald W., and Frances Ruane. 1990. "Appraising the Options for International Trade in Services." *Oxford Economic Papers* (November):672–687.

Jones, Ronald W., and Roy Ruffin. 1975. "Trade Patterns with Capital Mobility." In Michael Parkin and A. R. Nobay, eds., *Current Economic Problems* (Cambridge University Press); reprinted in abridged version in Ronald W. Jones, *International Trade: Essays in Theory* (Amsterdam: North-Holland, 1979), 207–225.

Jones, Ronald W., Isaias Coelho, and Stephen Easton. 1986. "The Theory of International Factor Flows: The Basic Model." *Journal of International Economics* 20 (May): 313–327.

Kemp, Murray C. 1966. "The Gain from International Trade and Investment: A Neo-Heckscher-Ohlin Approach." *American Economic Review* (September):788–809.

Kemp, Murray C., and Ken-Ichi Inada. 1969. "International Capital Movements and the Theory of Tariffs and Trade: Comment." *Quarterly Journal of Economics* 83 (August): 524–528.

Krugman, Paul. 1995. *Development, Geography, and Economic Theory.* Cambridge, Mass.: The MIT Press.

Kuhn, Peter, and Ian Wooton. 1987. "International Factor Movements in the Presence of a Fixed Factor." *Journal of International Economics* (February):123–140.

Lerner, Abba P. 1936. "The Symmetry between Export and Import Taxes." *Economica* (August):306–313.

Marjit, Sugata, and Hamid Beladi. 1998. "Complementarity between Trade and Factor Movement: Revisiting Mundell-Markusen Propositions." Unpublished manuscript.

Markusen, James R. 1983. "Factor Movements and Commodity Trade as Complements." *Journal of International Economics* 43:341–356.

Mayer, Wolfgang. 1974. "Short-run and Long-run Equilibrium for a Small Open Economy. *Journal of Political Economy* 82:955–967.

McKenzie, Lionel. 1954. "Specialization and Efficiency in World Production." *Review of Economic Studies* 21:165–180.

Metzler, Lloyd. (1949). "Tariffs, the Terms of Trade, and the Distribution of National Income." *Journal of Political Economy* 57 (February): 1–29.

Mundell, Robert A. 1957. "International Trade and Factor Mobility." *American Economic Review* 47:321–335.

Neary, J. Peter. 1993. "Welfare Effects of Tariffs and Investment Taxes." In W. Ethier, E. Helpman, and J. P. Neary, *Theory, Policy and Dynamics in International Trade* (Cambridge: Cambridge University Press), 131–156.

————. 1995. "Factor Mobility and International Trade." *Canadian Journal of Economics* 28:S4–S23.

Neary, J. Peter, and Frances Ruane. 1988. "International Capital Mobility, Shadow Prices, and the Cost of Protection." *International Economic Review* 29:571–585.

Nishimura, Kazuo, and Makoto Yano. 1993. "Endogenous Real Business Cycles and International Specialization." In W. Ethier, Elhanan Helpman, and J. P. Neary, *Theory, Policy and Dynamics in International Trade* (Cambridge: Cambridge University Press), 213–236.

Ohlin, Bertil. 1924. "A Theory of Trade." Ph.D. dissertation, Stockholm School of Economics; translated in Harry Flam and M. June Flanders, eds., *Heckscher-Ohlin Trade Theory* (Cambridge, Mass.: The MIT Press, 1991), 75–211.

Ohlin, Bertil. 1933. *Interregional and International Trade*. Cambridge: Harvard University Press.

Ohyama, Michihiro. 1986. "Protection and Factor Mobility." *Keio Economic Studies* 23:57–60.

————. 1989. "Factor Endowments and the Pattern of Commodity and Factor Trade." *Keio Economic Studies* 26:19–29.

O'Rourke, Kevin H., and Jeffrey G. Williamson. 1999. *Globalization and History: The Evolution of a Nineteenth-Century Atlantic Economy.* Cambridge, Mass.: The MIT Press.

Pennar, Karen. 1999. "From Here to There." *Business Week* (Collectors' Issue, Summer):37.

Purvis, Douglas D. 1972. "Technology, Trade and Factor Mobility." *Economic Journal* 82:991–999.

Ramaswami, V. K. 1968. "International Factor Movement and the National Advantage." *Economica* 35:309–310.

Ruffin, Roy. 1984. "International Factor Movements." In R. Jones and P. Kenen, eds., *Handbook of International Economics,* vol. I (Amsterdam: North-Holland), 237–288.

Rybczynski, T. M. 1955. "Factor Endowments and Relative Commodity Prices." *Economica* 22:336–341.

Samuelson, Paul A. 1948. "International Trade and the Equalisation of Factor Prices." *Economic Journal* 58:163–184.

———. 1953. "Prices of Factors and Goods in General Equilibrium." *Review of Economic Studies* 21:1–20.

———. 1971. "Ohlin Was Right." *Swedish Journal of Economics* 73:365–384.

Sanyal, Kalyan. 1983. "Vertical Specialization in a Ricardian Model with a Continuum of Stages of Production." *Economica* 50:70–88.

Sanyal, Kalyan, and Ronald W. Jones. 1982. "The Theory of Trade in Middle Products." *American Economic Review* (March):16–31.

Schmitz, Andrew P., and P. Helmberger. 1970. "Factor Mobility and International Trade: The Case of Complementarity." *American Economic Review* 60:761–867.

Spencer, Barbara, and Ronald W. Jones. 1991. "Vertical Foreclosure and International Trade Policy." *Review of Economic Studies* (January):153–170.

———. 1992. "Trade and Protection in Vertically Related Markets." *Journal of International Economics* 32 (February):31–55.

Stolper, Wolfgang, and Paul A. Samuelson. 1941. "Protection and Real Wages." *Review of Economic Studies* 9:58–83.

Svensson, Lars. 1984. "Factor Trade and Goods Trade." *Journal of International Economics* 16:365–379.

Tyson, Laura D. 1992. *Who's Bashing Whom? Trade Conflict in High Technology Industries*. Washington, D.C.: Institute for International Economics.

Uekawa, Yasuo. 1972. "On the Existence of Incomplete Specialization in International Trade with Capital Mobility." *Journal of International Economics* 2:1–24.

Venables, Anthony. 1999. "Fragmentation and Multinational Production." *European Economic Review* 43 (April): 935–945.

Wong, Kar-Yiu. 1995. *International Trade in Goods and Factor Mobility*. Cambridge, Mass.: The MIT Press.

Young, Allyn. 1928. "Increasing Returns and Economic Progress." *Economic Journal* 38 (December):527–542.

Index